WHERE HEROES TRAINED

The 736th Medium Tank Battalion (Special)

from its formation through secret battle training in the

DESERT TRAINING CENTER AND CALIFORNIA-ARIZONA MANEUVER AREA

February 1943–April 1944

DR. ROGER M. BATY and EDDIE L. MADDOX JR, EDITORS

Where Heroes Trained
The 736th Medium Tank Battalion (Special)

Published by Fenestra Books™
610 East Delano Street, Suite 104, Tucson, Arizona 85705 U.S.A.
www.fenestrabooks.com
Cover design and interior layout by Lunsford Graphics, Arlington, VA.

Publisher's Cataloging-in-Publication
(Provided by Quality Books, Inc.)

Where heroes trained : the 736th Medium Tank Battallion
  (Special) from its formation through secret battle
  training in Desert Training Center and
  California-Arizona Maneuver Area, February 1943–April
  1944 / Roger M. Baty and Eddie L. Maddox Jr., editors.
   p. cm.
  Includes bibliographical references and index.
  LCCN 2004109019
  ISBN 158736316X

  1. United States. Army. Tank Battalion Medium
(Special), 736th--History. 2. World War, 1939–1945--
Regimental histories--United States. 3. World War,
1939–1945--Personal narratives, American. 4. World War,
1939–1945--Tank warfare.   I. Baty, Roger M.
II Maddox, Eddie L., Jr.

D769.306 736th. W44 2004   940.54'1273
                QBI04-700300

Foreword

I am the son of 736th Tank Battalion veteran Eddie L. Maddox. I grew up with bits and pieces of stories about the "Special" Tank Battalion. My dad didn't talk much about it. He did wake up in the night and I could hear the end of his "bad dream," as he called it. As the years went by the dreams happened less often but I knew the cause. It was called "World War Two" to me. To him it was names, faces, and places. It was things I would never have to see, hear, or feel, thanks to him and his fellow soldiers.

In 1992, my father and I attended our first 736th reunion. From that point on the pieces began to fit together and the story of this battalion and its men came to life for me. In 1997, my father and I published a book entitled "736th Special Tank Battalion." It went through several printings. My dad passed away on February 13, 2002 and I continued to attend the reunions.

That year the reunion was held in Warner Robins, Georgia. It was my good luck to meet Professor Roger Baty of the University of Redlands. We had dinner and a brief conversation, followed up later by phone. I expressed my desire to help with the book he was preparing and agreed to be co-editor of "Where Heroes Trained."

I am pleased to be associated with the men of the 736th Tank Battalion and their families and it is a privilege to work with Roger. The 736ers and I are indebted to him for continuing to uncover and tell the story of these heroes of World War II.

God willing, we look forward to publishing another book, "Where Heroes Fought." This will follow the "Kid Battalion" across the ocean to Wales and finally into the European Theater of Operations, through the Battle of the Bulge and Ardennes, then on their mad dash across the Rhineland. This book will also combine records at the National Archives with oral history interviews.

Eddie L. Maddox Jr.

Acknowledgements

The editors received assistance from a number of individuals.
We thank our wives, Phebe Baty and Carol Maddox, who provide
unstinting support for our efforts. We also thank the following for
their encouragement and example:

The veterans of the 736th Medium Tank Battalion (Special), who
generously contributed their stories.

John Bennett, Robert "Bud" Wall, and the Bouse Chamber of Commerce,
for their vision and commitment to the veterans of Camp Bouse.

Donald E. Hunt, educator, companion through many adventures
in the desert, and organizer of the bivouac at Camp Coxcomb,
Desert Training Center.

Sandra Richey, Interlibrary Loan, Armacost Library, University
of Redlands, for never giving up on requests for fugitive material.

Dennis Casebier, Mohave Desert and Cultural Association, for his
personal example of caring for our desert heritage and sharing from
the fruits of his labor.

Mitchell Yokelson, for guidance through the maze of search aids
to find the treasures in the National Archives.

John S. Lynch (Lt. Col., USAF, retired), for pioneering efforts to
keep the military heritage of our deserts accessible.

Tom Hanchett, 526th Armored Infantry Battalion Historian, whose
documenting of military history through oral narratives serves as
an inspiration.

Les Scull, correspondent from England and veteran of the 49th Royal
Tank Regiment, for sharing the saga of his regiment and encouraging
our work.

Rudolf Dietrich, whose digital photographic assistance with restoration
and design add to the visual quality of the photos in the book.

Rolla Queen and those in the Bureau of Land Management who hold
keys to the preservation, enjoyment and interpretation of the Desert
Training Center/California-Arizona Maneuver Area.

Table of Contents

The Gizmo

(Photo courtesy of David Fletcher, Bovington Tank Museum)

Introduction to the Book

Analysis of reports from the battles raging in North Africa in 1942 had a direct bearing on the formation of the 736th Tank Battalion and the special role the Army trained it to perform. One requirement to defeat German armor was a more flexible armor formation than existed in the allied arsenal. Another observation was the German army did not fight well at night. In fact, the British reported no unsuccessful counter-attack when it followed the day's battle. This served to stimulate development of the secret night attack weapon implemented through the code name "Project Cassock."

The secret weapon was an M3A1 medium tank modified by replacing the 37mm gun turret with an armored searchlight. A high intensity carbon arc lamp generated a 13 million candlepower beam some 340 yards wide and 35 yards high at a range of 1000 yards (Hunnicutt, 1978). Fighter tanks and troops advancing in the "cloak of darkness" between the light tanks would see the battlefield clearly. Enemy troops would be dazzled like deer caught in a car's headlights. Detailed specifications of the weapon, known by the guys as the "Gizmo," are in Chapter Four.

To keep development of the weapon and the training of the men a secret, extraordinary measures had to be taken in order to ensure absolute security. This requirement also had an immeasurable effect on the lives of the men of the 736th. This book is their story, from the time of their first call-up through their training in remote and isolated parts of the United States. The stage is set with a sharing of family backgrounds. From there we follow them to Camp Rucker, Alabama, for Basic Training. Then the young professional soldiers move as a battalion to Fort Knox, Kentucky. From there they continue advanced battle training in the desert country of the California-Arizona Maneuver Area in western Arizona at a secret location designated Camp Bouse.

This is the story of training for the ultimate fight that never came. It is the story of taking boys leaving home for the first time and turning them into rugged and toughened soldiers ready for anything the enemy might throw at them. It is for another book to tell the story of what happened after their departure to the European Theatre of Operations (ETO).

This book depends on four main sources: personal visits to the training sites in the California-Arizona Maneuver Area (CAMA) and the town of Bouse, Arizona; oral history interviews with veterans of the battalion; research in the National Archives, College Park, Maryland; and the personal diaries kept by Jesse R. "Pete" Henson and Jack Gay. Pete salvaged his unpublished manuscript "My War" from the mud and debris which was all that was left of his home in Arizona after a devastating flash flood. His diary makes possible much of the continuity of our account.

CHAPTER 1
Family Backgrounds

Introduction

Most of the men who formed the 736th tank battalion were so young, they were referred to as "kids." In fact, that reference stuck and the entire battalion became known as the "KID BATTALION." That nickname is proudly referred to at each annual reunion.

These were ordinary kids. In this chapter we share something of their family backgrounds. They were from many parts of the United States. While they came mainly from the Midwest—states like Ohio, and Kentucky—there were others from Pennsylvania, Georgia, Minnesota, Texas, California and Washington. Not only were they from diverse geographic regions, their families reflected the range of economic opportunities available to working people at the time. They were farm boys, kids whose fathers were coal miners, sharecroppers, steel workers and railroad men. The parents of some were in the fishing industry, others in the timber business and still others in entertainment.

To a person they knew the meaning of hard work. Many had left school and were working when they received their call. Most had done some kind of work outside of school. "Pete" Henson had a job with the railroad. O.V. Coffman was in the building trade. Art Alexander had a job with Diebold Safe & Lock Company making armored plates for army half-tracks. John Mellon, the youngest kid in the battalion, was working in a steel mill.

They had no doubts about the rightness of the war they were drawn into. There was no questioning the authority of the government to call them up.

In this chapter we share family profiles of some of our interviewees. The photographs were taken near the time of enlistment or during training, prior to leaving for Europe.

ARTHUR L. ALEXANDER
Private First Class
35599807
7 September 1923
Waco, Ohio

My father was a blacksmith when I was young, then worked at Republic Steel. My mom was secretary for their church and a housewife. There were eight of us children—four boys and four girls. Me and my older brother were the only ones who went in the Army. Before going into the service, I was a single spindle drill press operator for Diebold Safe & Lock Co., Canton, Ohio. We worked on making the armor for US Army half-tracks. In terms of schooling, I finished ninth grade and "quituated." I left school and went to work at age fifteen. I got my induction notice on the twenty-first of January, 1943. I entered active service on the twenty-eighth of that month, at Fort Hayes, Ohio.

VERNE L. BROTHERS
Corporal, Tech/5
35599779
28 August 1923
North Industry, Ohio

North Industry is a little town south of Canton. My dad was a mail carrier. When I was born he was trouble shooter for Diebold Safe & Lock. But the family got to be bigger and he was always away so he took up mail carrying. My mother was a real mother, took care of all of us four kids. My brother Frank was two years older than me, they lost one between me and Bill, and Bill was four and a half years younger than me and they lost another baby and then Tom came along—he's eleven years younger than me. Frank and I were both in the war.

I was in the first teenage draft. I knew we were going to go. I was working at the Navy plant in Canton and I'd seen several shows and I wanted in the Air Corps. So I asked off one day from work and went to the post office and passed the eye test and one or two other tests, but I was under twenty one, this was in September or October, and I had to get my parents' signature. So I took that paper and put it in my lunch bucket. Well, my mother found the paper and she says, "What's the matter, don't you like your home?"

I hugged her and I said, "Mom, you're the best mom, dad's the best dad there ever was, but they're going to take me and I could get something I like."

She said, "Wait until they take you."
I said, "OK, I'll wait." So they took me in January.

CHALMER CHESTER "CHET" CLAPPER
Corporal, Tech/5
35599757
1 August 1923
East Canton, Ohio

I was born on a farm in East Canton. Never went in to hospital. My dad's name was Alph Terfield Clapper and mother was Emma Schram. Dad was from Robertsville, Ohio, and mother from Newbergh, New York. She was born here. Her parents were from Switzerland. Dad bought a farm outside of Robertsville, then bought another one next to it and kept 80 acres off the old one. It added up to 228 acres.

We farmed with horses. I was young when I learned to ride. We always had a couple of ponies. I used to go after the cows on the pony every day in the summer. We had wheat, oats, corn, about everything. We always had thirty to forty head of cattle to milk by hand. Twice a day. There were ten of us children in the family. One went into the service after I did, but that's the only one. Mother and dad were good farmers. They worked hard. When they cut corn, she was out in the field helping cutting. She would help with the milking. We walked two and a half miles to a one room school and had to do the milking before that.

What I learned on the farm that helped me when I became a soldier was respect for others. My mother and dad taught me a lot. "Do unto others as you would have them do unto you." Another thing was self-reliance. Don't depend on others. Don't lie, cheat or steal. The ten commandments. That was taught to all us kids.

O. V. COFFMAN
"Buck" Corporal
35694931
22 October 1923
Central City, Kentucky

My father, Raymond L. Coffman, was born in 1900 and passed away in 1989. He was a farmer by day and a coal miner by night for forty-eight years, under ground. My mother, Anna Swift, passed away in 1992 at the age of 84. She was a housewife. My folks separated when I was about five years old and I moved to Louisville where I lived with my mother and step-father. My mother and father would remain good friends until the day they died. My step-dad and dad were raised in adjoining farms. After I got out of the service I really got to know my real dad. I went to school in Louisville, did all of my foolishness and young teenage life—sowed my oats there in Louisville.

My mother was very strict because I lived in a rowdy Irish neighborhood. I was never in big trouble. When I was about eight years old, I sold newspapers on the corner of 7th and Oak St. in Louisville, was a soda jerker for Zegart's drugstore when I was about thirteen, also at 7th and Oak. I was raised to work, be honest and pay my debts and I've done that all my life and I've taught that to my children.

I went to 10th grade. In 1941 I went to work on construction. The first job I had was a carpenter's helper at Fort Knox. From there I was a truck driver. I helped build the gun powder plant over in Charleston, Indiana. I also helped build the bag plant where they loaded the charges in bags for the Navy big guns (155 howitzers) in Charleston.

Then I came back from there and I went to DuPont Neoprene, the synthetic rubber plant they were building here in Louisville. I worked for them about a year then I went to a company called Ford, Bacon & Davis, a contractor out of Texas and that's where I was drafted.

Gil and his brother at Camp Rucker

GILBERT GARCIA
Corporal, T/5
39277452
3 March 1923
East Los Angeles

I came from a family of thirteen. We were a very poor family. When I was in the 10th grade and had turned 15, I had to go to work part time and help support the family. My mother, my dad and my older brother were circus people. My mother and older brother were trapeze artists. My dad was a singing clown and also did a trapeze act with my brother.

I could walk on my hands pretty good, do hand flips, stuff like that. I guess I inherited from them, you know. My uncle never worked for nobody. He worked for himself. He was a very good hand ball player and they used to have tournaments in a big hand ball court. They used to come from Cuba and Puerto Rico. And my uncle used to be a candy man. He used to make Mexican candy and when I was a kid I used to go to the hand ball courts and sell the candies. I used to get a penny for every candy I sold that was a nickel. They used to call me the candy man. At the hand ball courts they used to pass a tray up and down the bleachers and when it come back, it come back with a bunch of nickels and no candy, see? I would get a penny for every nickel. My uncle also ran a pool hall, a billiard place, and I had a shine stand in the corner of this pool hall. I used to shine shoes. I used to shine shoes and also learned how to play pretty good pool.

I also caddied at the golf course when I was a kid. I remember one time for mother's day. I went to caddie because I wanted to buy my mother a box of chocolates I saw in a drug store down on Whittier Boulevard in East LA. And on the way back from the golf course I lost that one dollar I made in four hours. So I got my shoeshine box and went out, shined some shoes until I made enough to buy the box of candies. See, that's how much love there was.

JACK D. GAY
Private First Class
35770527
4 April 1925
Charleston, West Virginia

I was very athletic as a kid, played baseball, football and track. Was "churched." We went to Sunday school and church every Sunday. I wasn't a good student. I had a lot of fun and I didn't study enough to become really interested in an education and I doubt if I would have got a college education if it wasn't for the GI bill.

On the 4th of April, 1943, I became 18 years old. And on that day I registered for the draft as the law required. I didn't think too much about it as I and my parents felt that the board would let me finish my last semester which concluded in January, 1944.

I had one year of football. During that summer vacation I got a job at Owens-Illinois Glass Company. It was in the maintenance department. The deal was that I would work day shift, five days a week, off on Saturday and Sunday, and they would pay me 75 cents an hour. Mr. Butler, a member of our church, also informed me that they expected me to be the catcher on the company's softball (fast pitch) team in the city league. I accepted the job and went to work the following Monday. WOW! Seventy-five cents an hour! That was top money for a high school student. My first job. And I got it, and the money they paid me, as a result of a talent that I had in a sport. (Gay, *Family Story*, p.67, n.d.)

On July 19, 1943 I received my induction notice. This got our attention and for the next few weeks some serious work was done by Dad to see if the board would defer my induction into the service until after graduation. But they said, "You're not in school. You're working." So I went in service, and I didn't get to graduate.

Clayton, front row, center, with his Honor Guard buddies. Note how he is wearing his cap! Temperature in Alaska on this day was 20 degrees below zero! Photo date: Feb 2001

CLAYTON A. HELGESON
**Sergeant, T/4
19134222
27 February 1924
Montevideo,
Minnesota**

Both mom and dad came over on boat from Norway. There's a little bit of Swede in us (we don't mention that though). I was six years old when dad retired from the postal service. He had thirty years in there and we went to Washington. We drove all the way—five kids and mom and dad. He continued farming our place in Napavine, Washington. That's where I started in the first grade.

Our parents didn't have to tell us twice to do our chores, like getting the wood in, feeding the chickens, splitting kindling. Mom did her cooking on that wood stove. She was some cook. We really hustled with our chores so we could listen to the radio. Some of the programs were Jack Armstrong, and "Little Orphan Annie." We were worse than the kids today, wanting to listen to those programs!

I went to work there when I was in the sixth grade. Kept working for this guy. Must have worked there eight years. He had a chicken ranch with shrubbery and flowers and stuff. Kind of a nursery. He asked me to move there so I boarded there and moved in with him and his wife.

I graduated and my boss and my mom wanted me to go to college. And I didn't want to go. Anyway I went out to Pullman, Washington—Washington State College—and studied horticulture. I started in September and I didn't like it at all. I was eighteen then. That's when I told the woman there, "I quit." They said, "You go in the army."

JESSE R. "PETE" HENSON
Corporal, T/5
39854975
24 March 1923
Chillicothe, Texas

Photo: Winslow, Arizona, 12 November 1943, while on furlough from Camp Bouse

My mother and father were both raised in East Texas. My dad was raised in Bells, Texas, just outside of Dennison. My mom was raised in that area too, but out in the country. Mom's dad was a farmer. After my dad and mom got married they moved to West Texas. I was born in Hardeman County. My dad worked for the railroad then wanted to start farming. We were on the edge of the grass plains but not in the dust bowl.

When I was in the third grade we moved from Texas. We had been farming there and went broke in '31. We went out and picked cotton for 35 cents a hundred. That's slow money. Seventy cents a day for a big kid. It was so bad that my older sister was ready to graduate from high school and she had to quit school to feed the little kids, or try to. And we starved out. That was true of a lot of people. Most of them went to California. Dad had made a trip in 1927 to Arkansas. He was raised in east Texas where they had fruit trees and he just loved that Arkansas because like he said, "We can graze off the fence rows and eat better than we do here in Texas." So he sold everything we had, which probably didn't bring thirty dollars, but he was able to get a beautiful 1913 T model Ford with brass shell and the big headlights, and cut it up to make a four-wheel trailer out of it to haul our furniture. We had a Ford touring and an old Ford truck with ruxle rear end—2 speed rear end in it—just a T model. It made a pretty good truck. Smaller than a ton and a half is now but it still carried a load. And we pulled the four-wheel trailer behind the T model touring full of kids and furniture and the truck was loaded to the gills. We took anything in the way of food, bedding, clothes, and mom's older furniture that she'd had a while—dressers and things.

But Dad had already gone up there and he rented four, forty acre patches in this farm separated by road and he got it for 100 dollars a year—a big two bedroom house—huge barn, there were orchards, grape vineyards. He had seven boys and he put them to work!

We didn't make any money there but we sure ate good. He couldn't find any work at all around there but we went out in the woods and gathered wild walnuts, hickory nuts, wild grapes by the ton, and mom made grape jelly. We'd just barely have enough money to buy sugar and coffee and flour.

In Texas we lived close to a flour mill and we could get 48 pounds of flour for fifty cents. The sack made good dresses for the girls. The writing on it was made so it would fade right out with one washing and you got a real pretty piece of cloth. Mom made all the kids' clothes. We got a new pair of bib overalls and a pair of boy scout shoes every fall. Those shoes cost a dollar and twenty-nine cents. They were good sturdy shoes. We bought our clothes at Perkin-Watkins, like JC Penney. They had an ad showing a little black cat and it said "The cat came back and you will too."

The last place we lived we were twelve miles from town. To go to town—most of the time we didn't have a car that would run. Dad was a pretty good mechanic but he didn't have time to work on the car, he was farming. A lot of time we'd go to town on the wagon, usually with a load of cotton. Three hours. We'd unload the cotton and dad would want to go to the wagon yard and talk to his old horse-trading buddies. So we'd hang around there. One time he gave my brother and I a nickel and said "Go and get us a nickel's worth of cheese and crackers so we'll have lunch." And it was a huge sack! Loose crackers and good cheddar cheese. That was a feast to us. We ate beans–stuff we grew.

Another time I remember a whole hand of bananas. They were small but probably ten bananas on it and they cost a dime. Dad said, mama will raise cain about me spending this much money for lunch.We were so starved for fruit, my brother and I ate a banana and we had to save some for the little kids at home and we took the skin and would eat the soft inside of the skin. We didn't have a lot of sweets. About the only time we got candy was at Christmas. Dad managed to have Christmas candy.

EDDIE L. MADDOX
Corporal
34086870
2 August 1919
Hall County, Georgia

Eddie was born in Hall County, in Northern Georgia. When he was ten, the Depression began. As farmers, his family endured the bad times better than most. With the economy improving in the late thirties and early forties, his father turned from farming and opened a community store. Eddie and his identical twin brother Edward helped their father Walter Green Maddox at the store, but their fondness for automobiles received most of their attention. Eddie left for the CCC (Civilian Conservation Corp), and as only one family member could serve, he and his twin brother were for the first time apart. He drove a truck in Cherryville, NC and used his car as a way to make extra money, driving guys around on the weekend. When his time with the CCC was up he went back to the store. But his hometown seemed so much smaller and clerking at the store could not compete with big trucks and weekends in bigger towns. It wasn't long before he joined the Army.

Army life was just like the CCC until December 7th, 1941. He was at home that Sunday when President Roosevelt spoke to the nation. Dad packed his bags and said his goodbyes. My uncle, Dad's twin, told me, "I will never forget my brother running to his car and heading back to base."

JOHN P. MELLON

Corporal
13107982
15 February 1927
Homestead, Pennsylvania

Homestead was at one time home of one of the biggest steel works in the country. The town is separated from Pittsburgh by the Monongehala River. I lived for the first ten years of my life on a street which was two blocks away from the huge steel mill which loomed over us and which was central to our existence. My grandfather worked there, as did my father and uncle, as did most of the men who lived on our block, and as did I. During the twenties, there was great prosperity; huge amounts of steel were being produced for use by every segment of society; and men like my father worked long hours and were paid well enough to put down payments on houses. Ours was a modestly sized red brick one which had a view of the steel mill from the back windows.

When the thirties and the Depression arrived, our family, along with millions of others, suffered the consequences. Steel production was cut back severely, which made work scarce. Among my earliest memories was my father going down to the mill gate early in the morning and in the middle of the afternoon in the hope that he would "catch a turn," that is, be one of the few needed for work that day. Because he didn't catch many turns and money became scarce, he and my mother found it necessary to rent out the upstairs part of our house.

On one of the occasions when my father did work, he was severely injured when struck on the head by a steel beam being moved by an overhead crane. After a period of several months, it became evident that this formerly very active man would no longer be able to do what he did before. He was considered disabled and given a meager disability pension by the steel corporation. The desperate financial situation led to the selling of the house at a loss and a move to a subsistence level flat. At about the same time, my father's condition worsened enough to require that he be admitted to the county hospital. Although we visited him frequently, he never lived with us again.

It was up to my mother to find a way to support two boys, ten and seven, and herself. She had no education and no skills that would qualify her for work outside the house. At age 34, she began doing housework for others and continued to do so for many years. We survived. After Pearl Harbor, men were enlisting and being drafted right and left, thus causing a large problem for the steel industry. To keep up with the war effort, more workers were needed than ever before. In the winter of 1942, I was in the tenth grade and thinking about what I could do to help my mother with more than my paper route. Since I had already matured physically and was taken to be older than I was, I asked Mother if I could quit school and get a job in the steel mill. Desperate in her need of additional funds, she agreed. Forthwith, I was employed by the U.S. Steel Corp., giving my age as 18, so that I could work all three shifts, the second and third ones paying slightly more than the first. For the next four months, I performed hot and heavy labor tasks of one kind and another which had no redeeming qualities whatsoever.

When the draft age was lowered to 18 in June of 1942, and employees were required to show their draft cards, I promptly registered. I began hearing horror stories from my fellow workers about guys being drafted and sent directly to the South Pacific as sweating cannon fodder. I asked my mother if she were willing for me to enlist and to vouch that I was 18. I then went to the recruiting station to discover what opportunities would be available to me if I did join up. The recruiting sergeant went down the list, and when he reached "armed cavalry" I thought, "Oh boy, horses." I asked about benefits for my mother and brother; satisfied that they would be reasonably taken care of, I then signed up and was shipped to Fort Knox. There I began my army career at the ripe old age of 15—and never saw a horse.

JAMES H. MOON
Corporal, T/5
34824793
15 September 1924
Centerville, Georgia

Centerville is a little town about twenty miles from Atlanta, in Gwinnett County. My father was a sharecropper. People that owned the land would rent to my father and we would live on the property and farm the land and he'd get a small percentage of what he made. We grew cotton and corn. Growing up, I had chores to do. I had two brothers older than me and they did all the farm work. I was water boy. There was eight in my family. Three boys and five girls.

I worked on the farm until I went in the Army. So I didn't have too many hobbies. My two brothers did all the hard work. I just filled in with the soft jobs, more or less. We farmed with mules and when you'd get through plowing, you'd ride the mule in, back to the house.

I finished high school. I was drafted in January of 1943 and the Army gave me an extension until I finished high school. I graduated in June and was drafted July the tenth, 1943.

ROBERT V. OLSEN
**Sergeant
37316094
9 March 1922
New Ulm, Minnesota**

My family was in dairy farming. I have a son still milking cows. He's got about a hundred cows on the same farm. I grew up without electricity or running water on the farm. It was during the Depression. We didn't get running water until I got home from the service.

It was a mile and a half to school. One morning I fell through the ice. I kept paging through the school book I had so the pages wouldn't freeze, and I walked home and my mother took me to school. We always had work to do when we got home from school.

I had one brother and two sisters. My oldest sister worked for the War Manpower Commission during the war. My younger sister was a surgical nurse at the Mayo Clinic in Rochester. I was the oldest. I was drafted and my other brother stayed home for a while and helped my dad on the farm. But he wanted to go in the service so my dad let him go and he joined the 11th airborne, as a paratrooper. He went to the Philippines and the Pacific. He went to Tokyo the day the Japanese surrendered.

JOSEPH F. PERROTTI
Private First Class
35531448
21 June 1923
Cleveland, Ohio

My parents were living in Mayfield where most of the Italians were. They called it "Little Italy." From there they moved to the Collinwood area. That's where I was born. When I was about seven years old we moved to East Cleveland because that's where my dad worked. My dad was in the service department of East Cleveland. They picked up the rubbish and fixed the streets up, stuff like that. He worked for them for all his life. My mother was a housewife. She didn't have any time to go out of the house. Twelve children.

I was too small for sports in high school. In junior high school I played football; I was a guard. When the war came, I knew I had to go so there was nothin' else to do but do it. It was the first time I had been alone, the first time I left Cleveland except for a football game in Indiana. I graduated from high school and the day after I went into the army—whether I liked it or not, I had to go.

GILL W. TERRY
Private First Class
35531371
27 May 1924
Cleveland, Ohio

I have lived in the general area all of my life. My mother and father were divorced when I was a very young child and my mother and I went to live with my great aunt and uncle who worked for the post office. My mother re-married in 1938 and went to live in Detroit, Michigan. I continued to live with my great aunt and uncle until I went in the Army in January, 1943.

Gill during a weekend leave
from Fort Knox

Every summer when I was between the age of five and eight we spent several weeks at an island resort called Put-In-Bay which is located on South Bass Island in the western part of Lake Erie. Today this resort would be called a bed & breakfast. In those days they were called a boarding house. After my great uncle retired in 1932 the family leased a cottage on the island for the entire summer. This is where I learned to swim, fish, and shoot.

In high school I was too busy with automobiles and things like that to do much sports. I played a lot of intramural stuff but not with the high school team itself. I bought a car when I was pretty young. It was a 1934 Ford Roadster, for thirty five dollars, then after that I got a 35 Ford convertible which was really "cool" as they said in those days. At that time they used to have high school fraternities, at least in our area, so I belonged to one of those, and I met my wife in high school. We both went to the same high school and were in the same class.

Basic Training, Camp Rucker

VERNON L. TWEIT
Sergeant
39198815
8 June 1923
Bellingham,
Washington

My father passed away when I was five years old. I had a sister who passed away one year before my father. That left my mother with two of us to raise, my younger sister and myself. I don't know how she did it. But she did. She made maybe six or seven hundred dollars a year. She worked in the fish cannery and only when there was work available. That's all she had.

After I had graduated from high school, two men, I think they were Rotarians, came to the house to interview me and ask if I was willing to take the test offered for possible admission to West Point. At that time I wasn't ready to make that kind of decision, nor did I have being drafted or joining one of the services on my mind. I told them that I wasn't interested. I guess it could be said that I wasn't thinking too clearly.

I worked as a church janitor when I was in high school. My mother took over that when I went in the service. Big pay! That was fifteen dollars a month. Out of that fifteen dollars a month I managed to buy my first car—a 1923 Model T. Fifteen dollars I paid for that car. Then I graduated from high school here in 1941. Bellingham High School. Then I went to work in a grocery store.

In January 1943 I was called to report for the draft. On the 18th of January I was to report to the bus to be transported to Fort Lewis.

While we were waiting a list of names was read off and told to go home and report to the same place January 25. I was one of them. When I reported back on the 25th there were twenty five or thirty others there that were also being drafted. Some were from the previous week like me. We all got aboard the bus and I took my seat next to Jack Petersen. This was the first time I had met Jack. Others on the bus that were to become members of the 736th are:

Harold Weisenburger—dead
Frank Rucker—dead
Mel Gwinner—dead
Bill Eastman—dead
Jack Petersen—dead
Harley Peterson—dead
Joe Ferry—dead
Don Brighton—dead
Mel Johnson—dead
Myself—with Mel Johnson's death, I am the only remaining 736 member from Bellingham still living.

There was also one volunteer from Canada, Ralph Wherry, that has also passed away. He was from Victoria, B.C., Canada. He was trained as a Gizmo operator at the CCC camp at Ft. Knox. After we reached the desert he had a furlough to go home. He always said that the future of our Gizmo training depended on whether he returned or not from Canada. He said that he was told when furloughed that if he didn't return the project would be canceled. He returned.

CHAPTER 2

The Kids Leave Home for Basic Training

Introduction

Our heroes share very personal stories about a major change in their lives. Anthropologists refer to this experience as a "rite of passage." When a person changes from one social status to another there is a separation from the old status and a transition to a new one. The new status is often confirmed by receiving a document like a driver's license, or a diploma, or a wedding license. In the Army experience, separation comes with the letter of "Greeting." Separation intensifies when the young man reports to the induction center for physical and mental testing. When those tests are successfully passed, the separation is completed by taking the oath to abide by the uniform code of military justice. Everyone in the military has taken this oath or one like it. Now, the word "civilian" no longer applies. Now it is "recruit," or an even less impressive term, like "A-1 cannon fodder." The transition ends with graduation from Basic Training. The individual has earned the status of "soldier."

In this chapter our heroes share their stories of what must be one of the most difficult and challenging times in a person's life—the first separation from home. You will see why we thought of calling this chapter *You're in the Army Now!*

These kids were not surprised when they received their "Greeting." Some had been notified as early as September and everybody knew there was a war on. By mid-January 1943 teenagers were reporting to their induction stations. There the Medical Examination and Induction Board screened them to make sure they were fit to enter military service. They took a series of physical and mental tests. Those who passed were finger-printed and asked which branch of service they wanted to join. Of course, the actual assignment would depend on the needs of the military.

All these kids were classified as 1A. That meant they were sane, free of heart problems, hernias, venereal disease, poor eyesight, tuberculosis, or flat feet. They were not under-weight, over-weight, or illiterate. They had at least half of their natural teeth and were of the proper race. (At the time, under the "Jim Crow" practices in American society, the U.S. Army placed African Americans in segregated units mainly performing support and service duties).

After signing the induction papers, each man was issued a serial number and administered the oath. In unison, they repeated the following:

I _____ , DO SOLEMNLY SWEAR THAT I WILL SUPPORT
AND DEFEND THE CONSTITUTION OF THE UNITED STATES, AGAINST
ALL HER ENEMIES WHOMSOEVER; THAT I BEAR TRUE FAITH AND
ALLEGIANCE TO THE SAME; AND THAT I WILL OBEY THE ORDERS OF
THE PRESIDENT OF THE UNITED STATES AND THE ORDERS OF THE
OFFICERS APPOINTED OVER ME, ACCORDING TO REGULATIONS AND
THE UNIFORM CODE OF MILITARY JUSTICE. SO HELP ME GOD.

Then each enlistee received a sheet of paper with instructions detailing how they were to behave as a member of the "Enlisted Reserve Corps" before returning the following week for active duty. During the week at home they were ordered to "guard against disease, that might ruin my career and which I can avoid." Their instructions are quite personal and explicit. They help convey the nature of the changes ahead.

To be given to each inducted man and filled in by him prior to departure to the Enlisted Reserve Corps.

I am a soldier in the United States Army. I raised my hand today and swore that, "I would defend my country against all her enemies whomsoever." I now have new and different responsibilities. Today the Articles of War, the soldiers' law, were read and explained to me by an officer. I am subject to this soldier's law. I must obey, I must not bring discredit upon the military service because that isn't fair to the rest of the soldiers with whom I shall soon live. Even though I do not have my uniform, I am a soldier.

I, _____, have been sent to the Enlisted Reserve Corps and will be sent to the town of my local board. At the end of seven days I will report to my local board at 1440 Detroit Avenue at 11 AM on Jan. 29, 1943 for shipment to an Army Reception transferring me. My fare will be paid by the Army. I know that I must report to the local board at the hour and on the date specified. If I am sick or meet with an accident, I will notify my local board so the Army will know why I have not reported for duty. As soon as I am well I will report to my local board and my fare will be furnished.

One of the fellows has been placed in charge of the group. He didn't particularly want the job, but when he was appointed he took it. I am going to co-operate with him and that will make his job easy, and mine too. While I am at home I am going to protect my health. I will guard against disease, that might ruin my career and which I can avoid. When I report to my local board for shipment to the Reception Center, I will bring with me only a small traveling bag with a suit of underwear, and extra pair of socks and necessary toilet articles (razor, shaving cream, toothbrush, toothpaste, towel, face and bath.) The only civilian clothes I will bring will be the clothes that I wear, because when I arrive at the Reception Center I will have to send my traveling bag and civilian clothes home when my uniform is issued to me. When I am at home I will have my hair cut because the Army wants you to have your hair cut short. The Reception Centers are kept busy cutting hair of the soldiers who are stationed there permanently. I want to make a good impression. Having my hair cut, fingernails trimmed, presenting a neat appearance gives a good impression. I am going to do these things because first impressions are lasting. I am a soldier in the United States Army, as a reservist I will be strictly accountable, both personally and financially, for any damage to public property such as railroad, bus, hotel or restaurant, this includes all public or private property on the trip either from the induction station to the local board, or from the local board to the reception center.

**** I WILL REPORT IN A SOBER CONDITION AT THE RECEPTION CENTER ****

Oral Histories

Art Alexander recalls the time he was called up:

I knew about five guys who all went to school where I did. Jack Wireman, Verne Brothers, Jim Strader, Bob Corbit. We all went to the same school: Canton Township and later it was Canton South. There were no enlistments then. We were drafted. We all went to the induction center at Fort Hayes.

"Chet" Clapper relates his personal story.

I was called in September of '42 and went in, in January of 1943. I was drafted and took the exam in North Canton, Ohio. We went to Fort Hayes in Columbus for a couple of days where they decided where to send me. We were going through a line. I had a buddy who wanted the paratroopers. I wanted to be Air Corps, a tail gunner. They shipped my hide down to Alabama to a tank outfit. We were all young kids—eighteen years old.

Joe Perrotti told us there was no question in his mind.

I knew I had to go so there was nothin' else to do but do it. It was the first time I had been alone, the first time I left Cleveland. One time we went to a football game in Indiana, but we were always at home. I graduated from high school and the day after I went into the army, whether I liked it or not, I had to go. We went from Cleveland to Fort Hayes, in Columbus, and from there they sent you all over the country. We stayed there until they decided "You, you and you— you're going in the Air Force! You, you, and you, you're in the Infantry! You're going in a tank outfit!" I was lucky enough to go with the tank group. From Fort Hayes, we went to Camp Rucker, Alabama. Close to Enterprise.

Gill Terry, a Cleveland native, volunteered.

I wanted to do something, so that's what I did. I was inducted January 21st, 1943. I was in the first group of 18 year olds to leave Cleveland. I would have been drafted in March. A close friend of mine didn't volunteer and he was drafted in March and he ended up in a tank battalion also. The 712th tank battalion, which was part of the 90th Infantry Division. I think the 90th Division in Europe had more battle time than any other division in the European Theatre.

I went down to Fort Hayes, Columbus (Ohio). We were there for a short time, and from there went down to Camp Rucker, Alabama.

O. V. Coffman, an inductee from Kentucky, shares his feelings at the time.

In 1942 I got my greetings from my neighbors, telling me I had been selected—I didn't know I was that important. I cussed every one of them when I got home after I found out the situation, you know. When I went into the service we went up to Fort Benjamin Harrison in Indiana. We stayed there a day or so and they gave us shipping orders. We went up through Cincinnati on a train. They fed us there at the central station in Cincinnati. Then we came back down and I remember it was about midnight. We kept after the guy to tell us where we were going and he wouldn't tell us. I looked out of the window and we were crossing Broadway in Louisville. Me knowing Louisville like I did, I saw the mill, and I said, "We're headed for Fort Knox, bigger than heck." So I felt relieved and dozed off.

Well, when I woke up what a hell of a surprise it was. We were in a place I had never heard of—Ozark, Alabama. This was right out in a field, nothin' around us, all us kids lost, but we saw all these GI trucks there and the guys hollerin' at us "Fall in line!" "Git your duffel bags here!" So they load us on these trucks and they took us into this camp, Camp Rucker. Believe me, buddy, that was the tail hole of Alabama.

Clayton Helgeson had already signed up for ROTC.

I enlisted October 16, 1942. In January 16, 1943, is when I went in the service. I was at Fort Lewis, Washington, two days before they sent me down to Camp Rucker, Alabama. They wanted to get us as far away from home as they could possibly do and they did. We had a train ride all the way. They had given us a uniform and then we got more after we got to Camp Rucker. Naturally I got homesick. But we had a whole bunch of young kids there so we made out all right."

Vernon Tweit was also sent to Fort Lewis.

I was scared to death. I didn't know what I was getting into. I was called to be at the bus station to take the bus to Fort Lewis to be there on the 18th of January. I got to the bus station and some person came along and read off a group of names and said, "All you people go home and report back here on the 25th." One week later. So I got a one week reprieve there.

It was cold and snowy, I remember that. And they were parading us around Fort Lewis in that ice and snow down there, from building to building. They were outfitting us in clothes—throwing clothes at us—then they'd take us and get us something to eat and then they'd take us to our barracks. I don't know whatever happened to the clothes I wore down there. I never saw them again.

I was at Fort Lewis only about four days. Then they marched us to the train and we headed for Alabama. Along the way we stopped overnight in Chicago outside town in the stockyards. You can imagine what a night was like next to the stockyards in Chicago! We didn't have bunks, just our seats. It was a three or four day trip. We got to Alabama and debarked off that train in Ozark. They took us to Camp Rucker.

"Pete" Henson relates what the times were like.

I was always interested in the military. I used to go to the shows and see Fred McMurray as a young sailor. I had a brother-in-law that was in the National Guard, back when it paid two dollars a week. That's the only reason he was in there—to get that two dollars—because that was a lot of money. And they still wore the old wrapped leggings and the flat campaign hat from WWI. Then I had two uncles that were in WWI, one got blown up and lay out in a shell hole for two days with the leg bone completely off and lived. He was rich. He got nearly one hudred dollars a month for the rest of his life! No one else we knew ever had that much money. Then my Dad's youngest brother went over as an ambulance driver and he had a pretty rough time. He told me he killed a German with a pair of pliers. These Germans had broken through and one was coming at him with a bayonet and he jumped out of his ambulance and fought with him for a while and finally killed him with a great big pair of pliers. So those two kind of inspired me a little. I always wanted to be a soldier.

A year and a half before the war broke out I was in Winslow, Arizona. I lived with my sister until I got a job working for the railroad. At that time Winslow was the highest paid town in the United States per capita because of the railroad.

When the war broke out there were four of us who were nineteen and they were all between jobs or love affairs or something and we all four decided to join the army. We were going to join the army air corps. That was the big thing. You couldn't enlist then. You had to ask for voluntary induction through the draft board and the selective service system.

There was a lot of pressure. Even our girlfriends asked us, "When are you going? Aren't you going? Aren't you going to enlist?" There was peer pressure, social pressure. My mom and dad always believed whatever America wanted was fine. They supported us. Mom had four stars on her flag, one of them gold when my brother got killed in Italy.

I could have had a year deferment with my railroad job. But I turned that down. The four of us went over to the draft board at the county seat and they told us the air corps demand was filled, so they couldn't guarantee us the air corps. And Mrs. Towles that ran the draft board said, "You can go in now and take your chances. That will probably change next week. Or you can go back home. We'll be calling you within a few weeks anyhow." That's when I went back to tell my boss I was going.

I went to Fort MacArthur and the other two guys finally wound up with the mule artillery in Colorado. I got the tanks, which was my second choice. I liked it. If I'd got in the Air Corps then I'd been shot down in sixty days probably. That's when they were losing all the B-17's. And I'd have been a gunner. I told everybody I was going to be a tail gunner.

Gil Garcia also went to Fort MacArthur.

I wanted to go (into the army). I wanted to go. My brother told me that I could get out because I was the last boy in the house and I could get deferment from it. But I said, "No, I want to go, I want to go." And when I went to Fort MacArthur and they were calling all the names out, they were going to go to Dothan, Alabama. And they were calling all these guys that I knew from East L.A. and I thought, "Oh man, I hope they call my name." Well they did, they called my name and [chuckle]…and you know who I saw at the barber shop there at Fort McArthur when they cut our hair? Alan Ladd! He gave me a hair cut. But anyway you know they were very lonely nights for us over there. But like I said, see, I went in January, January the 18th. March the 30th is my birthday so, you know, usually when our birthday comes we have a big party for us guys, you know, at home. And that's what I missed, I missed the parties that mama did. We didn't have much money but she knew how to feed a bunch of us kids. They knew how to make a meal where it would stretch out.

I remember my dad saying, "Everybody sits at the table at the same time. I'm not running a restaurant, so come in late, you don't eat." But anyway, we got to Camp Rucker for basic training.

Fort McPherson, Georgia, was the screening point for some of the southern boys. **James Moon** was one of them.

I was drafted in January of 1943 and the Army gave me an extension until I finished high school. I graduated in June and was drafted July the tenth, 1943.

Although James went to Fort Knox, Kentucky for his basic training instead of Camp Rucker, the process was the same: show up, get tested, get issued some gear, and load on the train. That took two to three days.

James shared his feelings when he entered the Army.

I was proud. There was five of us from Stone Mountain that was drafted at the same time. We all went to Fort McPherson in Atlanta and every one of us passed the army test except one. He was so disappointed that he wasn't drafted. We were all in school together and we all wanted to go together. He was so disappointed, he went over to the Navy and the Navy took him. I don't know why he was rejected from the Army.

They processed us and issued our clothes and everything at Fort Mac. We stayed at Fort Mac about three or four days, I guess, before we went to Fort Knox. There was not one of them that went with me when I left Fort Mac and went to Fort Knox, Kentucky.

We rode a passenger train. This was before they had air conditioning. We loaded on the train about five o'clock in the evening. They were passenger train cars and we opened the windows and slept in the seats. Next morning we were covered with cinders from the train. Our khaki uniforms were the biggest mess you've ever seen.

Robert Olsen was processed in at Fort Snelling, Minnesota.

I was drafted into the Army October 12, 1942. I went to Fort Snelling, Minnesota, for the IQ tests and everything. Three of us went to Fort Knox from there. We took our basic training at Fort Knox, Kentucky. The others were from St. Paul. Most of them went to Camp Campbell, Kentucky. The only thing I remember is I had the papers and everything for it and we had pretty high IQ's. I don't know if it did any good. I was interviewed for OCS but they didn't take me and I didn't really care about going there either.

I had completed basic when I came through Rucker. When I got to Rucker they had only two tanks in our company (C Company). Hardly anyone had ever driven one. That's the only time I ever volunteered for anything. They wanted someone to teach tank driving. Which isn't such a complicated a thing to do for a farm boy, you know. That's what I started to do. I wanted to be a tank driver at the time.

We pick up **Jack Gay's** story with the news he got from his draft board that changed his plans for graduation.

On July 19, 1943, I received my induction notice. This got our attention and for the next few weeks some serious work was done by Dad to see if the board would defer my induction into the service until after graduation (Gay, *Family Story*, p. 68). But they said, "You're not in school. You're working." So I went in service, and I didn't get to graduate.

On August 9, 1943, my parents and one of my friends, Dave Sayre, saw me off at the train station in South Charleston. I really didn't think it was a big deal. That's why they were looking for a lot of eighteen-year-olders like me. We rode 60 miles west to Huntington, where we were taken to the Induction Center and put through a physical examination that I didn't have any trouble passing. They gave me my choice of armed services, and I chose the Army because if I ever got into a dangerous situation, I felt I could run faster and farther than I could swim.

We boarded another train and were in Ft. Thomas, across the Ohio River from Cincinnati, early the next morning.

There we received our uniforms and shipped our civilian clothing back home. The next day I was put on KP (kitchen police) and spent all the time I was on it opening number ten cans of beets and pouring the contents into huge cooking pots. It was long after I was married before I would eat beets again. From there I went to Ft. Knox, Kentucky, where I spent the next five months in the Armored Forces taking my basic training.

CHAPTER 3

The "Kid Battalion" forms at Camp Rucker, Alabama

Introduction

In January, 1943, the young men caught up in the first teenage draft began reporting to their places of enlistment. For many, this was their first time away from home. The kids came from several parts of the country. Sixty percent came from the Ohio region. Another contingent came from California. Georgia, Kentucky, West Virginia, Minnesota and Texas supplied the remainder. They came from urban, industrial, and rural, agricultural walks of life. Living through the Depression, they had one common denominator—their families took hard work for granted. O.V. Coffman's dad worked in the coal mines by night and farmed by day. Robert "Ole" Olsen's family were dairy farmers.

Some of the kids had already joined the work force. Pete Henson worked for the Santa Fe Railroad. Art Alexander was a single spindle drill press operator for Diebold Safe & Lock Co., Canton, Ohio. Some had not yet finished high school.

From their places of enlistment, they were sent to Ozark, Alabama, and trucked to Camp Rucker. Basic Training, or "Basic," began the process of changing these kids into trained soldiers, skilled at their jobs and ready to follow orders.

The postcard below was sent from Dothan, Alabama, December 28, 1942. It shows the Camp Headquarters. According to information from the Public Relations Office at the time, the Camp extended over 65,000 acres in the southeastern corner of the State. The camp's buildings were located in a triangle between the towns of Ozark, Enterprise, and Daleville. Within the boundaries of the camp is Lake Tholocco, which figures in one of the soldier's stories.

"Camp Rucker lies in a triangle formed by the towns of Ozark, Enterprise, and Dothan, in the southeastern corner of Alabama. Part of the reservation is a former government recreation area and contains a thousand acre lake which is now used for soldier recreation. One of the newest of Army posts, it was named after Colonel Edmund W. Rucker, an outstanding officer of the Civil War."

Postcard distributed by Dothan Cigar & Candy Co., Dothan, AL (R. Baty Collection)

Parent organization of the 736th

The parent organization of the 736th tank battalion was the 8th Tank Group. This organization began forming in the fall of 1942. On 10 August 1942, at Camp Rucker, Alabama, Lt. Col. Joseph H. Gilbreth assumed command of the 8th Tank Group under the provisions of Army Regulations 600-20. General Orders Number 2 from Headquarters, 8th Tank Group, dated 20 August 1942 at Camp Rucker, made the following assignments to the Staff of Headquarters, 8th Tank Group:

Commanding
LT. COL. JOSEPH H. GILBRETH, 016817, Inf

Executive and S-3
MAJ. FREDERICK J. SIMPSON, 018256, Inf

S-3, Air
CAPT. PAUL J. RITCHIE, 0302006, Inf

Major F. J. Simpson, the XO (executive officer) signed the order. All of these men were to play an important part in the formation of the special battalions including the 736th.

Formation of the 736th Tank Battalion

By 1 February 1943, the show was ready to start. General Orders Number 1 published at Headquarters, 736th Tank Battalion (M), Camp Rucker, announced the activation of the 736th Tank Battalion at 010001 hrs in accordance with Section III, General Orders Number 3, Headquarters, Armored Force, Fort Knox, Kentucky, dated 15 January 1943. Pursuant to the same General Orders, MAJ. WILLIAM H. DODGE assumed command of the battalion.

Three main objectives governed the Army's approach to Basic Training. First was military discipline. Second was protection of government property. The third was safeguarding military information.

Army Regulations No. 600-10 spell out in careful detail the meaning of military discipline.

> DEFINITION—MILITARY DISCIPLINE IS THAT MENTAL ATTITUDE AND STATE OF TRAINING WHICH RENDER OBEDIENCE AND PROPER CONDUCT INSTINCTIVE UNDER ALL CONDITIONS. IT IS FOUNDED UPON RESPECT FOR AND LOYALTY TO PROPERLY CONSTITUTED AUTHORITY. WHILE IT IS DEVELOPED PRIMARILY BY MILITARY DRILL, EVERY FEATURE OF MILITARY LIFE HAS ITS EFFECT ON MILITARY DISCIPLINE. IT IS GENERALLY INDICATED IN AN INDIVIDUAL OR UNIT BY SMARTNESS OF APPEARANCE AND ACTION; BY CLEANLINESS AND NEATNESS OF DRESS, EQUIPMENT, OR QUARTERS; BY RESPECT FOR SENIORS; AND BY THE PROMPT AND CHEERFUL EXECUTION BY SUBORDINATES OF BOTH THE LETTER AND THE SPIRIT OF THE LEGAL ORDERS OF THEIR LAWFUL SUPERIORS.

It took a while for this military discipline to become second nature. When the first of them began to arrive, there was a scramble to get organized and trained. Pete Henson recalls:

> To form the battalion, there were 80 of us from Fort MacArthur that went to Rucker. Probably half of these were Mexican Americans. (I was a little leery of them then, but now, the ones that lived are my friends). We were raw recruits. They hadn't even taught us how to salute yet. We got down there and here's an outfit that has half the officers there and the rest of them haven't been assigned yet! We got a cadre of non-coms from Fort Knox and they had to pull KP! We needed the basic training so badly that they wouldn't give us KP.

Vernon Tweit commented that basic training "started out by teaching us our left foot from our right foot!" He added, "A lot of nomenclature, machinery, weapons, but it was a lot of teaching us coordination. It was just parading and a little weaponry but mostly orientating the guys to army life. Learning who you're with. Meeting your neighbors."

There were personal relations that had to be established. Chet Clapper relates an experience that shaped his relationship with another soldier for the entire war. Chet complained that "a lot of guys didn't even have respect for others. It's a shame. Maybe it's the way they grew up." One incident came to mind during our interview.

> There was one big guy in the outfit and every time we'd come in the barracks, he'd run into you and say, "Watch where in the heck you're going." Or something like that. I didn't want to foul up getting into the army and I never said nothin'. But he was doin' it every day. He was about twice as big as me. One day I was on KP and I had a pretty hard day. I never came in the barracks until 8 o'clock. I'd no more than started walking through the barracks and down he come, walked right into me and knocked me over. Knocked me down. I come off the floor and I hit him so far that I knocked him down and jumped on top of him. I was just so mad at him. Afterwards I was sorry I done it, but I knocked the heck out of him. I was pretty wiry then. He never bothered me since then. He was a big guy.

O.V. Coffman tells the tale this way:

> We went through basic training there and we had latrine duty and didn't know what a latrine was. We were just kids, babies, no fuzz on our face, but it didn't take long for us to get out of that. We started doin' double-timing and road marches and then after a small time we started learning how to field-strip guns, .30 calibers and things of that nature. And we had to do it blindfolded because our work mostly was in tanks in dark where you had to do this thing in the dark.

> It wasn't too long until they issued us tanks. You talk about a bunch of happy guys when they assigned us a tank. They just looked like big monsters to us. Each crew, five men to a crew, we had to go in and get all the equipment out and this was all in cosmoline, waterproofed for shipment. So we had to get all of that cleaned off and that was a job. We did that, then we started our driving and regular training with them, learning the

nomenclature, how the guns worked and how to use them. When they got us all assigned, I was assigned as a gunner. We had a gunner, a driver, a bow gunner, loader and tank commander. These were the M4 Sherman tanks.

Some had an edge on parts of the training because of what they learned back home. Gil Terry remembers, "I already knew how to shoot pretty well, because I'd done quite a bit of shooting when I was a kid. I could already shoot a gun. I was not used to big caliber guns so they taught us how to shoot big guns and machine guns, how to march, do KP, and clean the garbage cans."

In addition to training, there were social obligations and introductions to the Camp Rucker community. The *Camp Rucker Reporter* published an informative description of the 736th, soon after it formed up. Gil Terry kindly provided us with this clipping. Included in the report are the names of all the officers of the unit.

MAJOR WILLIAM H. DODGE, COMMANDING

Capt. George P. Callison, S-2, S-3
Capt. Maurice H. Rahe, adjutant S-1
1st Lt. Mordie I. Garber, S-4
Capt. John F. Loeck, Bn Surgeon

1st Lt. Joseph T. Matson, commanding Headquarters Company
1st Lt. Leo J. McCarthy, commanding A company
1st Lt. John C. Allan, commanding B Company
1st Lt. Glynn O. Rogers, commanding C Company
1st Lt. Willard L. Thompson, commanding Service Company
1st Lt. Clyde C. Glindmyer, Bn Maintenance officer
2nd Lt. James C. Bergin, Personnel officer

Second Lieutenants were mainly platoon leaders.
Those joining the unit were:

Donald R. Allen	Woodrow W. Bobo	John Coveney
Henry J. Fleagle	Richard E. Fox	Silas E. Gochnour
Paul J. Heaven	Blaine S. Irish	James D. Janes

Clifford O. Johnson	Karl K. Koppa	Paul E. Lassen
Joseph G. London	Richard D. Maier	Henry J. Mieczynski
Conwell Myers	Burton C. Potter	Hugh G. Rowland
Jerald S. Ruckman	John M. Stormy, Jr.	Robert H. Taylor
Charles R. Van Hoesen	Charles A. Watson	

FRIDAY, FEB. 26, 1943

736th Tank Bn. Hold First Social Event At Rucker

Officers and wives of the newly activated 736th Tank Battalion (M), were honored recently with a dance given by the 8th Tank Group in the mess hall.

The first social event for the new Battalion, the dance served to introduce to the group 23 officers who had joined the 736th since its activation February 1.

Commanded by Major William H. Dodge, the 736th Tank Battalion is the youngest tank outfit on the post. On activation it was attached to the 8th Tank Group.

Hosts at the dance were officers and wives of the 8th Tank Group Headquarters, the 746th Tank Battalion (M), and the 748th Tank Battalion (M).

Officers who have joined the Battalion since its activation and who made their initial appearance socially with the group included Second Lieutenants Donald R. Allen, Woodrow W. Bobo, John Coveney, Henry J. Fleagle, Richard E. Fox, Silas E. Gochnour, Paul J. Heaven, Blaine S. Irish, James D. Janes, Clifford O. Johnson, Karl K. Koppa, Paul E. Lassen, Joseph G. London, Richard D. Maier, Henry J. Mieczynski, Conwell Myers, Burton C. Potter, Hugh G. Rowland, Jerald S. Ruckman, John M. Stormy, Jr., Robert H. Taylor, Charles R. Van Hoesen and Charles A. Watson.

Moving rapidly into the full swing of training, the 736th Tank Battalion—little more than two weeks old—has already completed more than a week of its regular training schedule.

Receipt of fillers—the 18 and 19 year-old variety—three days after activation, made possible the opening of a full training schedule. Today the Battalion moves under a full head of steam aiming at a new high in the way of training records and successes.

Officers with the battalion at activation included: Major Dodge, commanding; Capt. George P. Callison, S-2, S-3; Capt. Maurice H. Rahe, adjutant; 1st Lt. Mordie I. Garber, S-4; Capt. John F. Loeck, Bn. Surgeon; 1st Lt. Joseph T. Matson, commanding Headquarters Co.; 1st Lt. Leo J. McCarthy, commanding A company; 1st Lt. John C. Allan, commanding B company; 1st Lt. Glynn O. Rogers, commanding C company; 1st Lt. Willard L. Thompson, commanding Service Co.; 1st Lt. Clyde C. Glindmyer, Bn. Maintenance officer; 2nd Lt. James C. Bergin, personnel officer.

Soon, the battalion was beginning to shape up. Their training program was accelerated. And because of special circumstances which none of the enlisted men and few of the officers knew about, the men were training with others who would be permanently part of the same unit. In retrospect, all would agree that they were lucky to be part of a unit that stayed together. Some of the men never made permanent membership in the unit. The search for blabbermouths was underway.

Training took on deadly serious dimensions. Chet Clapper recalls the gas chambers.

> We had gas chambers. I went to the school of chemical warfare. One out of each company had to go to that there school and I was picked in my company. We went through the chambers and all the different gasses. Tear gas. It would make you cry. The right name for that is "chlorasetta phenoon." Our purpose mainly was to make sure they knew how to put the mask on and be prepared for it, because there are so many different gasses. Mustard gas will blister ya. I knew them gasses forwards and backwards when I went there. The purpose was to come back and train the rest of the company.

Art Alexander commented on the importance of getting cross-trained. "We had to do all five jobs: driver, assistant driver, gunner, and loader, and tank commander. We had to know all them jobs in case one was knocked out, you'd know how to take his place. We were training on Shermans."

What was really being taught, Joe Perrotti recalls, was discipline: "I think the first thing you had to learn, you had to learn to take orders. You had to learn to listen to those in command, and what they told you, you had to do. You couldn't question anything because they had the stripes and everything and we were just 'buck-ass privates.' We learned how to take orders from people and do it the right way."

Another military objective was the protection of government property. This was accomplished by posting guards at critical locations. Each soldier had to memorize eleven general orders:

(1) TO TAKE CHARGE OF THIS POST AND ALL GOVERNMENT PROPERTY IN VIEW.

(2) TO WALK MY POST IN A MILITARY MANNER, KEEPING ALWAYS ON THE ALERT AND OBSERVING EVERYTHING THAT TAKES PLACE WITHIN SIGHT OR HEARING.

(3) TO REPORT ALL VIOLATIONS OF ORDERS I AM INSTRUCTED TO ENFORCE.

(4) TO REPEAT ALL CALLS FROM POSTS MORE DISTANT FROM THE GUARDHOUSE THAN MY OWN.

(5) TO QUIT MY POST ONLY WHEN PROPERLY RELIEVED.

(6) TO RECEIVE, OBEY, AND PASS ON TO THE SENTINEL WHO RELIEVES ME, ALL ORDERS FROM THE COMMANDING OFFICER, OFFICER OF THE DAY, AND OFFICERS AND NONCOMMISSIONED OFFICERS OF THE GUARD ONLY.

(7) TO TALK TO NO ONE EXCEPT IN LINE OF DUTY.

(8) TO GIVE THE ALARM IN CASE OF FIRE OR DISORDER.

(9) TO CALL THE CORPORAL OF THE GUARD IN ANY CASE NOT COVERED BY INSTRUCTIONS.

(10) TO SALUTE ALL OFFICERS, AND ALL COLORS AND STANDARDS NOT CASED.

(11) TO BE ESPECIALLY WATCHFUL AT NIGHT, AND DURING THE TIME FOR CHALLENGING TO CHALLENGE ALL PERSONS ON OR NEAR MY POST, AND TO ALLOW NO ONE TO PASS WITHOUT PROPER AUTHORITY.

Not surprisingly, there were some unofficial versions of some of the orders. One that comes to mind is, "I will walk my post in a military manner and take no crap from the company commander."

But the duty was taken seriously. Part of military discipline meant that all soldiers, no matter what their rank, had to respect the members of the guard as they performed their duties. Any suspicious-looking person and all persons involved in disorderly conduct were to be arrested. Not only were the sentinels required to patrol their post in a prescribed manner, they also had to be constantly alert and observing everything taking place within sight or hearing.

Instructions for guard duty were quickly prepared. As early as February 5, 1943, soldiers were "pulling" guard duty. The guard organization consisted of one officer of the day, one sergeant of the guard, three corporals of the guard and six privates or privates first class serving as sentinels.

The normal tour of duty was 24 hours. Reliefs were normally on post two hours and off four hours. They wore the "C" uniform with full field equipment, less musette bags. The individual small arms were normally the Thompson Sub-machine gun for the sentries and .45 caliber pistol for officers and non-commissioned officers. The General Orders Number 2, February 5, 1943, instructed sentinels, while on post, to keep their weapon loaded, but not with a round in the chamber unless it became necessary to fire the weapon. Upon return to the guard house, all ammunition was removed from weapons.

The members of the guard had responsibility to enforce uniform regulations and to be sure that vehicles were parked only in authorized areas. Field Manual 26-5 laid out how the duties would be performed. The privates of the guard were instructed to challenge during the hours of darkness. The General Orders instructions stipulated that "Suspicious persons, or persons unknown to the Sentry whom he observes in the Battalion Area in civilian clothes when not accompanied by a member of the Battalion will be required to have a pass signed by the Adjutant or other competent authority."

Each soldier memorized the General Orders and had many turns at guard duty. Knowing the General Orders really paid off for one of the guys, Gilbert Garcia, from East Los Angeles. His experience is a miracle and might not have happened if it weren't for guard duty and knowing his General Orders.

Gil recounts one time when he was pulling guard duty.

They used to give us a stick to walk guard duty, he explained to Eddie Maddox in the interview. I was walking guard duty with this other young guy and I see this guy about a block away.

I say, "He sure looks like my brother." Eddie, he had been gone for two years! I kept looking and looking and the more I look, I say, "That is my brother!"

He came to me and he tells this other buddy. "Look what they're bringing us to fight the war now, these kids!" Now of all the camps in the United States…I run into my brother in Camp Rucker Alabama!

And my brother says, "Let's go to town."

I say, "I can't go to town because I'm not finished with my basic."

He says, "We'll go talk to your Commanding Officer." (1st Lieutenant Joseph Matson.)

We went in and talked to Lieutenant Matson and I said, "This is my brother, haven't seen him in two years and here I run into him here in Camp Rucker. We would like to go and take a picture and send it to my mother."

The lieutenant says, "Do you know general orders?"

I say, "Yes, Sir." So I give him my general orders.

So he says, "OK, I'm going to let you go for one night. You can go downtown for one night."

We went down to Dothan, Alabama. We took a picture and sent it to mama. Things like this don't happen that you run into your brother in the whole United States you know. But anyway…those were my lonely days. Like I said, Eddie, we used to go to town and get in the bus and be coming back to the camp and, O man, I would…I would really be…home sick. *(The photo of Gilbert and his brother is in Chapter 1 of this book. Editor)*

Of course, there were illnesses. Gill Terry recalls:

At one time there was a big confab and as a punishment they made everybody go on a twenty-five mile hike, at night time. It was raining. I had a pain on my side and they took me in and discovered I had appendicitis. They took my appendix out.

In those days they didn't get you up out of bed like they do now, so I ended up getting pneumonia. I was laid up for about a month and then I was sent home on sick leave. I weighed about 110 pounds when I got home, so I missed a lot of things. I was gone almost two months. You might say it set me back.

In thirteen weeks, the men knew a lot more about themselves and each other. They also knew something about how the army worked informally and how to have some fun in spite of all the regulations. Art Alexander remembers a work detail that Bob Hall put him on.

Bob had a clipboard and rounded up several of the guys and said, "You, you, and you, come with me, I've got a detail." It was Glen Host, Bob Bean and me. He marched us out of there and down to the woods and we went down to a crick for swimmin'! I'll never forget that as long as I live. We went down to the woods and come to an opening. Sun was shining right through these trees. Here was a great big snake. Seven foot long. It was a rattler. He was curled up and we jumped back and he started uncoiling. We had a long dry stick and we struck at the snake. Bob Bean took the snake and was going to skin him and make a belt out of it. I don't think he ever did. That was a good experience. I wasn't too interested in going in the water.

Sometimes they could leave the camp and visit one of the towns nearby. Art continued:

Enterprise was the little town near the camp. I went down into the town and I heard people hollerin' like hell, and wondered what was goin' on. Here a colored guy got on the sidewalk and these white people down there kicked his rear end for bein' on the sidewalk. He wasn't allowed on the sidewalk. That was them days. And on the bus, if a guy got on he'd have to move to the back. February, 1943. That's how it was down in Alabama.

The town itself was not exactly demonstrating "southern hospitality" to the troops, either. Joe Perrotti recalls, "We'd go into town once in a while and they had coffee. Ten cents for civilians and soldiers, twenty five! They were making a killing when the GI's went in town."

Morale-wise, they learned some songs along with the general horseplay that turns strangers who left home for the first time into comrades ready to go to the ends of the earth together. One of the songs, "When They Tried to Make a Tanker out of Me," they sang to the tune of "John Brown's Body."

> Oh, they took me up Snow Mountain just to learn me how to drive,
>
> Oh, they took me up Snow Mountain just to learn me how to drive,
>
> Oh, they took me up Snow Mountain just to learn me how to drive,
>
> When they tried to make a tanker out of me.

Chorus

> Glory, Glory what a hell of a time they had,
>
> Glory, Glory what a hell of a time they had,
>
> Glory, Glory what a hell of a time they had,
>
> When they tried to make a tanker out of me.

The first lines of the rest of the story follow:

> We were coming down Snow Mountain when the damn thing threw a track....
>
> Oh, the air was blue with cussing when the Sergeant found it out....
>
> Oh, they put me on the garbage truck to teach me double clutch....
>
> Oh, they sent me to the radio school to teach me dits and dahs....
>
> Oh, they sent me to Cooks' and Bakers' School to teach me how to cook....

Another one, "The Tanker's Song," they sang to the tune of "Clementine."

> I'm a tanker, I'm a tanker,
>
> Glory be to God on high.
>
> When there's trouble, we're on the double,
>
> To keep this land forever free.

I'm a rough guy, I'm a tough guy,

There is nothing that I fear,

When there's trouble, we're on the double,

To keep this land forever free.

We are tankers, we are tankers,

And when we throw life's mortal track.

All the angels up in the heavens,

Will greet the tankers, welcome back.

An amusing incident involving their battalion commander, Major Bill "Wild Bill" Dodge, comes from Pete Henson.

> Wild Bill was a drinking man and loved to chase the nurses when in his cups. The Battalion had obtained an amphibious peep called a seep *["peep" is a tanker's name for a jeep, Ed.]* and when it had been used in the water, two big bilge drains had to be left open so the hull could drain and dry out. On a Sunday afternoon, Wild Bill took a nurse down to the motor pool, loaded her in the seep, and took off for the lake. When he arrived, without checking anything, he pulled out in the water and went winding his way merrily across the lake. He realized something was wrong when the water came up over his feet. Before he could turn around and return to shore, the seep had gone to Davy Jones' Locker in about 10 feet of water. Luckily, both occupants could swim, and they got out of the water in good shape. Monday morning, Maintenance had to raise the seep, drain all gear boxes, the crankcase, the hull, and dry out the ignition to get it going again. (Henson, "My War," p.27–28)

By the time they were ready to leave Camp Rucker, there were already signs that something special was afoot for the 736th. Some of the recruits who were not getting with the program disappeared, perhaps sent to other units where the conditions facing them would be less exacting.

Here is what was happening behind the scenes. While they were being called up and run through Basic Training, the Armor leadership at Fort Knox was designing a special weapon for fighting the decisive battle against the Germans. These raw recruits, on their way to becoming soldiers, were destined to become one of six elite armor battalions (approximately 720 men each) to receive training on this weapon. By the time the outfit left Camp Rucker, their future had already been determined.

While researching this story, accounts from some of the other battalions have come to light which help us understand what was happening behind the scenes at the officers' level. Almost fifteen years after this decision took place, Lt. Stuart L. Daniels, Intelligence Officer (S-2) for the 748th Tank Battalion, recorded his memories of the events involving the 748th. His article, "The mystery of our most secret weapon," was published in the *American Weekly*, August 11, 1957. In Lt. Daniels' words,

> *In February, 1943, at Camp Rucker, Alabama, I was called into a behind-closed-doors meeting with Lieut. Colonel Robert I. Glass, commanding the 748th Tank Battalion. I, along with other battalion staff members, was told we had been selected for a top secret project, the nature of which could not yet be revealed. All the officers present swore, on oath, that we would never reveal to any person what we were about to learn.*
>
> *During the next few weeks I assisted Colonel Glass in screening our personnel. Almost 100 men were transferred to other units. These were the unreliable, the blabbermouths, the excessive drinkers, the low I.Q.'s, and foreign-born soldiers with relatives living under enemy control who might be coerced into giving information.*
>
> *Then, our security belt tightened, we entrained for Fort Knox, Kentucky, home of the Armored Force.*

So the 748th Tank Battalion departed for Fort Knox and the 736th soon followed, but not before some last-minute "stress-relieving" behavior at the local PX. J. R. "Pete" Henson has kindly given us permission to quote from his unpublished manuscript entitled "My War" which he salvaged from a devastating flood that destroyed his home in Arizona. His story takes us from the last days at Camp Rucker, Alabama by railroad to Fort Knox, Kentucky.

On June 9, the Blue Flag went up over our headquarters, signifying an imminent move.

On June 20, 1943, we loaded our barracks bags for shipment to Knox, keeping what we had to have for the trip in our musette bags. We then went to the PX and proceeded to tank up. The 746th and the 736th got into a fight that turned into a riot. The battalion guard was called out, and the OD (Officer of the Day) got slugged right in his cigar. There was a big, round table with lots of full beers on it, and Sgt. Laymon and I grabbed an arm load of beer and got under the table where we sipped our beer and watched the fights. They finally got everyone out and closed the PX; then, several fights erupted up and down the street. "A" Co., which wasn't much involved, had guards all up and down the street to separate the battlers.

On June 21, 1943, which was a Monday, we fell out, policed up the area, then changed to suntans, with full field equipment. I was picked for train guard and changed back into "C" uniform with steel helmet and a brand new M-l Tommy gun. It was a very enjoyable trip, riding the flat cars or up in the vehicles when it rained. We ambled all over the country with us guards flirting with the girls and snowing the boys in the towns through which we passed. When we arrived at Birmingham, we laid over in a rainstorm for nine hours and never did learn why the delay.

The men in the chair cars were certainly jealous of the men on guard as we were the only ones to get any cool air. We would change guards on the run when we slowed in some town, then, if possible, we could take a nap with three men in a chair car seat. Once, we thought we were in Tennessee, but during the night, we had turned and wound up in Mississippi. We stopped in Corinth, where the company fell out for calisthenics in the heat. I was sure glad I was on guard.

*We next stopped at Fulton, Kentucky, where there are lots of
pretty girls, then on to Paducan, the home of Irvin S. Cobb,
where the guards dismounted and patrolled the train. I got to
talk to some local girls there. During the night, we passed over
a river, where a huge dam was under construction and reached
Ft. Knox at daybreak.*

*I had been relieved at 0100 and had tried, without success,
to catch some sleep in that hot, old, chair car, then stood guard
from 0800 till 1100, while the train was being unloaded, and
really felt bad. It was so hot and sultry, and we only had two
barracks and had company mess, eating out of mess kits. I had
been on guard for 49 hours and was filthy; couldn't get a
shower till 2300 that night.*

CHAPTER 4

Project Cassock and the Canal Defense Light

Months before activating the 736th tank battalion, the Army was considering a secret weapon that would take fighting to the enemy during the night when he was most vulnerable. The first large scale demonstration of this weapon was at Lowther Castle near Carlisle, England on May 5, 1942. Viscount Alan Brooke and Earl Mountbatten viewed the tanks in action. Later in the year, several months before Operation Torch, when Rommel was still leading the Afrika Korps, the British Army invited the top American military commanders to observe another demonstration of this secret weapon they labeled the Canal Defense Light, or CDL, for short. The British pinned high hopes on this weapon and began development of tactical doctrine using the Matilda, a tank that fought with infantry.

They put on quite a show for the American and British top brass at Lowther Castle and invited the Americans to become involved in the top secret effort they dubbed "Project Cassock." General Eisenhower was impressed enough to have his staff recommend that "Cassock" be considered by the U. S. Army.

Note: The following quotation is from the secret files of the United States and British Armies based on information supplied by officers connected with the project. The material was obtained by Dr. Baty at the National Archives and is now declassified by authority NND88750. The portions of the document photocopied do not contain a date, but internal references suggest it was compiled up to and during the fall of 1943. We quote here from the first pages of the report.

History. (From secret files of this headquarters and information furnished by officers connected with the project.)

(1) The project, originally known as C.D.L. and code named "Cassock" for the U. S. Army, was developed by the British and demonstrated to a selected group of United States Army officers at Lowther Castle in the vicinity of Carlisle, England, during the fall of 1942. The officers included in this group were General Eisenhower, General Clark, General Barnes, Colonel Frank Reid, Colonel Ray Cochran, Colonel Torrence, Colonel Ennis, and Colonel Alger.

(2) As a result of the original demonstration and further investigation by staff officers, ETOUSA, it was recommended to the War Department by General Eisenhower's headquarters that "Cassock" be considered by the United States Army. The War Department accepted the recommendation and requested that a limited number of sets of this equipment be immediately procured and shipped to the United States.

(3) During December 1942, it was recommended by ETOUSA that a senior officer and three or more highly qualified enlisted personnel from the Armored Force be sent to England to take instruction in Cassock with a view to forming a cadre for a similar school in the United States. Colonel F. M. Thompson and three enlisted men from the United States were sent to England and were joined there by Captain J. S. Avent, Captain J. R. Kirwan, and Lt. C. B. Kelton, selected from a replacement center in England. These officers and two of the enlisted men took the course at Lowther Castle, England, and in addition several officers were sent for specialized instruction to various manufacturing centers in the United States, where component parts of Cassock equipment were to be made.

In a letter dated February 5, 1943, Lieutenant General Jacob L. Devers, Commanding General of the Armored Force at Fort Knox, Kentucky, conveyed his recommendation to Lieutenant General Lesley J. McNair, Commanding General of the Army Ground Forces.

This letter was a follow-up to a plan submitted to General McNair's headquarters on January 29.

HEADQUARTERS ARMORED FORCE
OFFICE OF THE COMMANDING GENERAL
FORT KNOX, KENTUCKY

Classification cancelled ~~~~~~~~~~~~~~~~~~
by authority of *Ab2 1 st 3rd 51 jan* by ....
on *11 March* 194 6......

BOICE R. KIZER,
C.W.O., U.S.A.,

February 5, 1943

Lieutenant General Lesley J. McNair
Commanding General, Army Ground Forces
Army War College
Washington, D. C.

Dear Les,

    Based on my observations of CDL equipment in England, I am satisfied that the project has many potentialities which we should explore. While the basic tactical doctrines for employment of the equipment should be worked out here at Fort Knox, I believe it would be wise to send the first two battalions trained in the school here to the Desert Training Center to work with divisions and develop tactics for employment on a large scale.

    My staff agrees with the British that two battalions of CDL will furnish the proper proportion for an armored division. The Desert Training Center, at the proper time, should work out the proportions for other type divisions.

    It is, therefore, recommended that early consideration be given to the plan submitted to your headquarters on January 29 (now in the hands of Colonel Ennis, G-3 Section, AGF). Adequate facilities for the technical and theoretical training of CDL operators can be provided at Fort Knox with a minimum of overhead and expense. It is believed that the plan submitted is in sufficient detail to indicate our ideas on the conduct of this training.

    I am all set to go on this whenever you say the word.

With kindest personal regards.

Sincerely,

JACOB L. DEVERS,
Lieutenant General, U. S. Army,
Commanding.

1

CEDAR CREEK

With the approval of General Devers' recommendation, Fort Knox became the location for the CDL Training Center with a staff of 18 officers and 59 enlisted men. By mid-February, the 375th Engineer Battalion was building the infrastructure for the training center at a location called "Cedar Creek." The engineers cleared out an area which had been used as a tent city and built a more permanent facility. This included construction of water storage tanks, a mess kit laundry, a sewage system, and water supply lines from storage tanks to the kitchens and latrines. They erected 40 buildings for barracks and instruction and fenced the entire area.

Cedar Creek after project completion. Photo courtesy of
Carsie Denning Sr., official photographer of Project Cassock

MISSION OF THE SPECIAL TRAINING GROUP (STG)

The mission of the CDL Training Center was to train individual soldiers and tank crews in the operation of the CDL equipment. This involved theoretical, mechanical and technical training. The training would provide men who could operate as single vehicle crews and also as a platoon. This would be the fundamental building block for later training at the company and battalion levels somewhere else.

To accomplish the mission, the Training Center staff generated a fifteen-day course in two parts. Part One consisted of nine days of technical and mechanical classroom work. Part Two involved six days of practical field work. The men would learn the theory of operation as well as the practical application in a combat situation. "By lecture, demonstration, and application, to completely indoctrinate the trainee with the effectiveness of C.D.L. operation and instill in him an enthusiasm for its use. By practical work in the field, in the use of combat C.D.L. equipment, to establish the basis for the continuation of C.D.L. unit and combined training." (Incl. #2, C.D.L. Training Center Mission and Scope. National Archives, RG 337.)

A board of officers consisting of Lt. Gen. Devers, Maj. Gen. Barnes, Colonel Thompson, and Captain John Savage was appointed to meet in Detroit, Michigan on February 19, 1943. There they were to make recommendations to the Chief of Staff on whether CDL equipment might be produced in the United States for employment by the United States forces. They were also to recommend the quantity of production if they decided to go ahead with it.

This board recommended the formation of ten battalions and the manufacture of 825 leaflets (the code name for the CDL tanks). Captain John Savage was tasked to serve as coordinator between Fort Knox and the Tank Automotive Center in Detroit.

Soon sixteen M-3 American tanks with British special equipment had been delivered and put in use at Fort Knox. Two pilot sets of special equipment manufactured in the U.S. were tested and found satisfactory. Both British and American equipment had one optical chamber in each tank. The production schedule called for 500 American "leaflet" tanks with American-made special equipment prior to 1 July 1944. Production until 20 October 1943 was to be two units per day with plans to increase that to three units per day after 15 November 1943. By increasing the production to four units per day, the total run could be completed by 31 March 1944.

They anticipated that this schedule would allow for 108 Leaflet tanks (enough to equip two battalions) by 15 December 1943. "The total number of tanks allotted for this project will equip two groups of three battalions each as now organized under T/O 17-25 and will leave an excess of 176 tanks. If special training is limited to one group headquarters and four battalions now set up for special training, an excess of 284 tanks will be available as replacements." The report also noted that the M-3 medium tank would retain its 75mm gun.

Specifications of the M3A1 tank (after Gander, 2003; and Hunnicutt, 1978)

Remanufactured to CDL configuration by American Locomotive Company
Designation: Shop Tractor T10
"American Locomotive delivered the first T10 in June 1943 and had converted 355 by the end of the year. An additional 142 were completed in 1944 for a total production of 497 U.S. CDL tanks. Both M3s and M3A1s were used for the U.S. vehicles." (Hunnicutt, 1978,p.397).

GENERAL DATA

Crew of five		Driver, front center of hull
		Gunner at driver's right
		Tank comander left of driver
		Loader behind the gunner
		CDL operator in turret
Weight		58,900 pounds (unstowed)
Length		222 inches
Width		107 inches
Height		123 inches
Track (tread)		83 inches
Track width		14 inches
Ground clearance		17 inches
Maximum speed, level road		21 miles/hour
Range, road		about 120 miles
Maximum trench		7.5 feet
Maximum vertical wall		2 feet
Minimum turning circle (diameter)		62 feet
Maximum grade		60 per cent
Engine	Make and Model	Wright (Continental) R975 EC2
	Type	9 cylinder, 4 cycle, radial
	Weight	1137 lb, dry
	Fuel	92 octane gasoline, 175 gallons
	Engine oil	36 quarts
Transmission		Synchromesh, five speeds forward, one reverse
Steering		Controlled differential
Suspension		Vertical volute spring
		12 wheels in 6 bogies
Electrical system		24 Volt DC

ARMOR AND ARMAMENT

Hull thickness	Front, Upper 2.0 inches
	Sides: 1.5 inches
Primary Armament	1 x 75 mm M2 gun in sponson on right side of tank with traverse of 14 degrees each side; Gun mount fitted with an auxiliary rotor shield to improve armor protection;
Secondary Armament	1 x .30 caliber machine gun in front plate
	1 x .30 caliber Browning machine gun in ball mounting in turret

Specifications for the CDL turret

Builder: Pressed Steel Car Company
Lamps: Mole-Richardson Company
Final assembly: Rock Island Arsenal

Turret configuration	Two compartments separated by armored bulkhead
	Left compartment for operator who also manned the machine gun
	Right compartment for the high intensity carbon arc lamp
Turret armor	Cast steel sides 2.55 inches thick with rolled plate top bolted in place
Turret traverse	Manual
Carbon arc lamp	13 million candle power
Power supply for arc lamp	10kilowatt DC generator and regulator at left rear of hull compartment driven by power takeoff from engine
Light slot	Vertical slot 24 inches high by 2-3/8 inches wide
Beam dimensions	340 yards wide and 35 yards high at range of 1000 yards
System optics	"The heart of the system was the mirror which was parabolic in the vertical plane and elliptical in the horizontal plane. With this arrangement, a carbon arc at the focal point produced a normal searchlight beam when viewed from the side, but in the horizontal plane the light passed through a second focal point 60 to 70 inches from the mirror. A flat aluminum reflector directed the beam from the parabolic-elliptical mirror toward the front of the turret where it passed through a vertical slot located at the second focal point. Thus the high intensity beam was brought out through a narrow slot with practically no loss of light." (Hunnicutt, 1978,p.395)

The report also decreed that "units committed to this project are screened and frozen prior to indoctrination. Individuals who become partially incapacitated during training are utilized in service functions in the two training centers, and those who are totally disabled will be held in designated hospitals."

The Army personnel working on this project had a number of other irons in the fire. They had to continue coordinating with the British. They had to find a suitable place for advanced training at the company and battalion level. Crucially, they had to keep the whole project a secret.

COORDINATION WITH THE BRITISH

The British had three training installations where they experimented with CDL equipment. There was the CDL School at Lowther Castle, Penrith, England, with responsibility for technical development and basic and technical training in the CDL.

The 79th Division, Linney Head, South Wales, had responsibility for experimental and tactical development of the CDL. The Middle East CDL School and Training Unit was responsible for Basic Training and tactical development of the CDL.

These schools devised a system of liaison between them through a series of monthly letters and reports. A similar system was set up to communicate between those in England and the CDL Training at Fort Knox. Liaison also took place between the British Army Staff through the British Ministry of Supply Mission in Washington, D.C. In this manner they ensured that CDL training would be working from the same "sheet of music" on both sides of the Atlantic.

ADVANCED PLANNING FOR A FOLLOW-ON TRAINING SITE

Efforts to find a suitable place for follow-on training considered at least two sites—one in Wyoming and the other in the Desert Training Center in California. In a secret memorandum for Col. E. K. Wright, Chief of Staff, Armored Force, Col. F. M. Thompson, and Lt. Col. Robert R. Glass, 748th Tk Bn (Sep), concurred in their recommendation that the Pole Mountain Area in Wyoming was unsuitable for Advanced Cassock Training and suggested "that further consideration be given to an area in the Desert Training Center." (Memorandum dated May 10, 1943. National Archives, RG 337.)

At this time the Desert Training Center was in full swing as the primary training area for armored and armored infantry divisions. On June 28, 1943, a secret directive was dispatched from Headquarters Armored Force at Fort Knox to the Commanding General, Army Ground Forces, Army War College, Washington, D.C. (General McNair). This endorsed an investigation and reconnaissance of the northeast section of the Desert Training Center, which was carried out in collaboration with the Commanding General, Desert Training Center. The endorsement recommended an area to be used by Cassock battalions. All civilian activities were to be removed from the designated area. A semi-permanent camp would be established in the vicinity of Butler Well, "originally for two tank battalions, one armored infantry battalion, and a group headquarters, with a view to expansion to six tank battalions, one armored infantry battalion, and a group headquarters." Section "e" in the endorsement recommended that a well or wells northwest of Cunningham Wash and in the vicinity of the power line be developed to produce 75,000 gallons of water per day. Section "f" recommended that one reinforced engineer company of the 20th Armored Division be sent to the Desert Training Center without delay on temporary duty with the mission of constructing:

1 building 20 x 100 feet (office)

1 building 96 x 160 feet (maintenance shops)

1 building 48 x 98 feet (storage of
special equipment)

1 building 20 x 100 feet, modified (small parts
storage and school)

Necessary screened mess halls, latrines,
and bath houses

High barbed wire fence for tank park and
maintenance shop area

The endorsement continued with requests for necessary telephone connections and a ten-car railroad spur at Wenden as a railhead. [*The railhead was later changed to Bouse. Had this not happened, the Camp might have been named "Camp Wenden" instead of Camp Bouse, since camps were often named after the closest railhead. Ed.*]

At this time, late June 1943, they envisaged a training cycle of three months and requested that an armored infantry battalion be sent, followed by the 748th Tank Battalion and then the 736th Tank Battalion. They also asked authority for early activation of an Armored Group (Separate) (Special) in accordance with a chart they had submitted to AGF on 24 June 1943. (4th Endorsement, Headquarters Armored Force, Fort Knox, Kentucky, 28 June 1943. Signed by Major T. E. Sims, Assistant Adjutant General. National Archives, RG 337.)

Earlier in the month, plans for Cassock Training were finalized. Six battalions would receive technical training at Knox, with advanced tactical training probably in the Desert Training Center (DTC).

This final advanced phase of training would provide for combined training with specially selected infantry or armored divisions.

The following memorandum provides insight regarding the scope of the planning:

HEADQUARTERS ARMORED FORCE
Office of the A. C. of S., G-3
Fort Knox, Kentucky

June 4, 1943

MEMORANDUM FOR: G-4, Armored Force.

1. The present plans for Cassock Training are set up about as follows:
   a. Six battalions to receive technical training at Knox.
   b. On completion of technical training at Knox, each battalion to be moved to an advanced (tactical) training center (probably in DTC area) and trained under our supervision.
   c. Final phase of training to provide for combined training with specially selected infantry or armored divisions.

2. We have estimated that one Cassock Battalion could support a division. Therefore, we can assume that the six battalions being trained could cover a continued front of six divisions or approximately 10 - 12 miles. Actually they would probably be utilized on more than one front.

3. The Supply and Maintenance problems of this project will increase as equipment and training increase and must receive a major amount of pre-planning prior to the combined training stage. It is recommended that arrangements be made to train a minimum of one maintenance company concurrently with the second or third battalion receiving technical training.

4. I have asked Col. Thompson to provide you with the special T/0 for the type battalion.

E. K. WRIGHT,
Colonel, GSC,
AC of S, G-3.

FINALIZING SECURITY ARRANGEMENTS

The last major component of Project Cassock in place before the troops arrived from Camp Rucker was the security situation. The Americans took their lead from the experience and recommendations offered by Colonel Ollington, British Army. Col. F. M. Thompson, Commanding the Special Training Group, received verbal approval for his plan for the Special Training Group (STG) from Brigadier-General David G. Barr, then Chief of Staff in mid-March 1943.

This plan began with the need to provide instruction to the officers and men as to the need for secrecy, the penalties for violations and a severe restriction of the men from any outside contacts for a two-month period. In a letter he wrote to the Commanding General, Armored Command, Fort Knox, Colonel Thompson explained the rationale for the two month period of restriction:

> "It is believed that individuals are more apt to talk of something that is new to them than something that has become common place due to the passage of time. The period of two months was selected as adequate to complete instruction in secrecy and allow the project to lose its initial interest in the mind of the individual. To further help in the security, permission has been granted to allow soldiers to explain their work by saying that they are being instructed in the use of tanks for air field defense. The dual responsibility of secrecy has been stressed whereby one must prevent his fellows in the project from talking as well as guard his own speech." (Letter dated 29 November 1943)

The legal foundation for Army action was the Espionage Act of June 15, 1917. This act details all sorts of actions that counted as unlawfully obtaining or disclosing information affecting the national defense. Penalties ranged from fines not to exceed $10,000, or imprisonment for not more than two years, to imprisonment for not more than thirty years, or death. For immediate reference, all commissioned personnel of the STG were to become familiar with the provisions of AR 380-5, "Safeguarding Military Information."

On March 31, 1943, Colonel Thompson forwarded a detailed plan for STG security to the Chief of Staff. In this plan he clearly states that the security of secrecy of projects is a command function and therefore the responsibility of all echelons of the chain of command. He also declared that "Battalions undergoing training will conform to the secrecy regulations of the [Special Training] Group. All members of the battalion undergoing training will be initiated to the project. The maintenance of secrecy within that part of the battalion not quartered within the training area is the responsibility of the battalion commander." (Thompson Memorandum to Chief of Staff, March 31, 1943.)

Implementation began through secrecy security education of the officers. In addition to AR 380-5, they had mimeographed material for informal presentations to the men on topics including espionage, sabotage, arson, counter-intelligence, and Fifth Column activities. They secured the following films:

TM 11-205	"Safeguarding Military Information"
TM 11-321	"Combat Counter-Intelligence"
TM 11-225	"Interrogation of Prisoners"
TM 11-325	"Safeguarding Classified Material"
TM 30-938	"Mr. Blabbermouth"
TM 30-947	"Don't Talk"
TM 30-950	"Next of Kin"

They also encouraged reading on counterintelligence problems in general. Copies of the Secrecy Security Education Program for Officers were sent to the STG and to the 748th Tank Battalion, the first battalion to receive the special training.

With these plans in place, the cadre of the Special Training Group prepared to "welcome" the unsuspecting soldiers fresh out of basic training at Camp Rucker.

CHAPTER 5

Advanced Training:
Fort Knox, Kentucky

Introduction

In early June 1943, the army was making final decisions that would affect the destiny of the "Kid Battalion." One record from the National Archives appears to be of a phone conversation between Colonel R. F. Ennis, G-3 Section, Hq. Army Ground Forces (AGF) in Washington, D. C. and Colonel E. K. Wright, GSC, Assistant Chief of Staff, G-3, Armored Force, Fort Knox, Kentucky. According to this record, by 4 June 1943, six battalions were listed for eventual use as battalions for Cassock training.

Colonel Wright recorded that tank battalions were being set up for several purposes. A decision was made to list the following battalions as "the only battalions available" for Cassock training:

748th Tk Bn, M	750th Tk Bn, M
736th Tk Bn, M	740th Tk Bn, M
749th Tk Bn, M	701st Tk Bn, M

The record candidly states that "this list is only tentative as requirements for battalions will undoubtedly upset this schedule." In fact, the 749th and 750th Tank Battalions (M) received other orders. They were later replaced by the 738th and 739th Tank Battalions.

Reflecting its new mission, the 736th Tank Battalion (M) was redesignated and reorganized. Effective 21 June 1943, the battalion became the 736th Tank Battalion Medium (Special). The notice of redesignation and reorganization was issued as General Orders Number 6 from the Headquarters of the 736th Tank Battalion

Medium (Special) at Fort Knox on 1 July 1943. It was by order of Lieutenant Colonel Dodge and signed by James C. Bergin, 1st Lt., Battalion Adjutant.

On that same date, 21 June 1943, Colonel Thompson, commanding the STG, dispatched his Bi-weekly Report to the Commanding General, Armored Force. He indicated that the training program for the 748th Tank Battalion (M) (Sp) would conclude on 29 June 1943, and school training for the 736th would start on July 5 and conclude around August 20.

Although authorized thirty leaflet tanks, Col. Thompson noted only five were on hand, plus ten turrets sent over from England. These would be stripped for school purposes. He expected two models with the American-made equipment on or about July 7. They would use these for tests as well as for instruction in regular school training. *[It is possible that our cover photo of the M3 with the CDL turret is one of these tanks. Ed.]* "Ten tanks without turrets but modified by the American Locomotive Corporation and Rock Island Arsenal are expected on or about July 15, 1943. Thus two tanks without turrets will be available as spare vehicles. In the event of serious mechanical breakdown, turrets can be transferred."

Two remaining tasks needed urgent attention: determining how to manage the trainees at the Special Training Group site on the fort; and designing procedures for ensuring secrecy.

The 748th Tank Battalion was the first unit to wrestle with management of the troops in an environment of ensuring secrecy. Their experience helped shape that of successive battalions. A memorandum prepared for battalion officers laid out the management plan in a detailed list of thirty specific instructions. This was published at the end of the 736th's cycle on 30 August 1943.

MEMORANDUM: Instructions for Officers of Trainee Battalions at Special Training Group Area.

TO: Officers, Trainee Battalions.

1. Check to ascertain that all Officers and enlisted Men have taken the oath upon their arrival at Special Training Group area. The Adjutant, Special Training Group, will administer the oath to those who have not taken it.

2. Have copies of all orders placing officers and Enlisted Men on Special Duty with Special Training Group delivered to Headquarters Special Training Group on same day as reporting for duty.

3. Officers arriving at Special Training Group for training report to the Adjutant, Special Training Group for assignment of quarters.

4. Enlisted Men arriving at Special Training Group area report to Orderly Room for barracks assignment.

5. Keep record by name of men in each barracks occupied by personnel of trainee battalion.

6. Appoint sufficient mail orderlies to assure prompt delivery of mail to each barracks occupied by personnel of the trainee battalion.

7. Meals—Week Days, breakfast 7:00 A.M., dinner, 12:00 noon, supper 5:30 P.M. Sundays, breakfast 8:00 A.M., dinner 12:00 noon, supper 5:00 P.M.

8. Outgoing mail leaves Headquarters, Special Training Group at 8:30 A.M, and 1:30 P.M. daily, except Sunday. Incoming mail arrives at Headquarters, Special Training Group at 11:45 A.M. and 4:45 P.M. daily (except Sunday).

9. Enlisted personnel of the trainee battalion will not bring private cars, etc. to the area, and, if possible, they will be given ample opportunity of arranging personal affairs prior to their arrival at Special Training Group Area.

10. No passes or furloughs will be issued enlisted personnel of the trainee battalion after arriving at the Special Training Group area. Officers can obtain a pass only from the Adjutant, Special Training Group.

11. Officers of the Day and members of the guard will be furnished by the trainee battalion. Copies of guard orders can be obtained from the Adjutant, Special Training Group.

12. Officers of the trainee battalion are welcome to enjoy the privileges of the Special Training Group Officers' Club during their stay in this area. A copy of the By-Laws is posted at the club.

13. Athletics are encouraged. Athletic equipment may be obtained from the Recreation Hall attendant. Areas for seasonal sports are located in the area.

14. Up-to-date movies are shown on the average of five nights weekly in the Recreation Hall.

15. A circulating library is located in the Recreation Hall consisting of modern literature suited for various tastes. Books can be obtained from the Recreation Hall librarian.

16. The Commanding Officer of the trainee battalion detachment in the Special Training Group area will report promptly to the Special Training Group Fire Marshall for information relative to fire fighting details, area fire regulations, etc.

17. Drivers of all vehicles will be cautioned not to exceed 10 M.P.H. in the Special Training Group area.

18. Post Exchange hours are from 11:00 A.M. until 9:30 P.M. daily.

19. Military courtesy and discipline of enlisted personnel should not be allowed to become lax.

20. For information as to time classes begin, student routine, etc., contact Special Training Group S-3 for details.

21. Constructive criticisms are welcomed at Headquarters, Special Training Group.

22. No personal telephone calls will be made by enlisted personnel of the trained battalion unless monitored by an officer of the Special Training Group. This does not apply to calls made in line of duty.

23. Enlisted Men's mail will be censored prior to leaving the Special Training Group area. Letters, etc., will not be mailed outside the area and will not be accepted for mailing if sealed. The Officer of the Day will not [act] as censor for battalion outgoing mail. Officer's mail will not be censored.

24. Police of the area will be accomplished by the trainee battalion except around those buildings occupied by personnel of the Special Training Group.

25. A list should be prepared of the duties to be performed by all personnel of the overhead, by name, and submitted to the Adjutant, Special Training Group. This is for the purpose of facilitating the issuance of Special Training Group passes to such personnel to permit entry into the Motor Park of truck drivers, tank drivers, maintenance men, etc.

26. Secrecy in matters concerning the project will be continually impressed upon Officers and Enlisted Men of the trainee battalion.

27. Daily disposition report (details, etc.) will be delivered to Headquarters prior to 9:00 A.M. daily except Sunday.

28. On the last day of stay in the Special Training Group area Officers will submit in writing to the Special Training Group Adjutant criticisms designed to improve the presentation of instructions.

29. Turn in all passes issued by Special Training Group prior to departure.

30. The old and new Officer of the Day will report, in the uniform of the guard, to the Commanding Officer, Special Training Group at 11:30 A.M. daily. Report will be formal. In the absence of the Commanding Officer, report will be made to the Executive Officer, or, in the absence of both the Commanding Officer, and the Executive, to the Special Training Group Adjutant.

By order of
Colonel THOMPSON, ROBERT G. HISEY, 1st Lt. Inf, Adjutant

A summary of this list shows at least nine different areas where the officers had management responsibilties:

Security (1, 26, 11)

Reporting (3, 4,16, 27, 30)

Control of Movement (2, 5, 9, 10, 17, 25)

Communications (6, 8, 22, 23)

Scheduling (7, 18, 20)

Recreation (12, 13, 14, 15)

Care of the facility (24)

Feedback (21, 28)

Military Discipline (19)

The second task was to determine how to solve the security issues. First Lt. Stuart L. Daniels, Adjutant for the 748th Tank Battalion, drew up a plan for security based on the 748th's experience. On 29 June 1943, this plan was forwarded to the Commanding General, Armored Force, Fort Knox, with Endorsements by Colonel F. M. Thompson, STG, and Lt. Col. Robert R. Glass, Commanding the 748th Tank Battalion (M) (Sp).

SECRET   **SECRET**   **SECRET**

S-1, S-2, STAFF STUDY
SECURITY AND SPECIAL TRAINING

INTRODUCTION:
748th Tank Battalion (M) (Sp) having been designated to perform a special mission and having been charged with the responsibility for security within the command, has found that many existing regulations and rules of administration hinder the security of the mission and obstruct the precise safeguarding of specific military information.

PRESENT SITUATION:
1. It has been determined by careful observation and study that the only way to maintain absolute security is to restrict the contacts that members of the organization have with civilian and other military personnel. To this end the following rules have been established:

   a. No enlisted man leaves the organization area without a companion who remains with him at all times.
   b. Informal censorship of outgoing mail has been established.
   c. No individual furloughs are granted. Any man leaving on furlough must have another enlisted man of this Battalion with him.
   d. All members of the organization are under careful surveillance.

ANALYSIS:

1. However, all precautions even the use of a secluded training area are nullified by the following conditions:

   a. A certain number of men develop physical or mental ailments which require hospitalization.
   b. These men are often recommended by hospital disposition board for discharge under the provisions of Section II or Section VIII of AR 615-360.
   c. Men whose physical or mental disability places them on limited service.
   d. Men who are charged under the Articles of War with serious offenses and punishment is prescribed as confinement in a post stockade.
   e. Men who go A.W.O.L. and are not recovered in sufficient time to determine whether they have violated security rules.
   f. The necessary morale factor of granting furloughs and still remain consistent with security precautions.

2. Since the security policy set down is to keep any person familiar with or cognizant of the nature of the special training apart from all other personnel, military or civilian, the above "human elements" have developed difficulties in following the security program. This security program means almost absolute isolation for any person engaged in the project. To this end, this organization will move to an isolated area in the near future. Other organizations undergoing this training will follow.

3. Any and all of the conditions mentioned above tend to place the personnel mentioned in contact with persons unauthorized to receive information of the nature involved. While it is probable that the intense security program will "keep the mouths shut" in most instances it is also probable that the individuals mentioned such as the physically or mentally incompetent, the rebellious or insubordinate type and A.W.O.L.'s cannot reasonably be presumed to be able to keep quiet.

4. As an example: One soldier has already been charged and tried on a violation of his oath to keep secret certain information. He carelessly revealed secret information and was tried. While his violation warranted a more severe penalty, the only practicable penalty was restriction for the maximum allowable time. If a penalty such as confinement was prescribed the man (already known to have violated security) would be removed from the control of this organization, and placed in contact with unauthorized persons.

5. Through circumstances beyond our control it is reasonable to presume that the next few months will see certain individuals placed in Limited Service or dischargeable categories; disciplinary cases will arise, emergencies necessitating furloughs will arise.

RECOMMENDATIONS:

1. This organization is the first of many to undergo this special training. As the number of persons involved increases, the possibility of leakage of information will also increase. Without a clearly defined policy whereby any given circumstance that arises may be handled, all of the expense, time and effort involved may become worthless. It is important to note that secrecy and the continued security of the project are as important to its ultimate success in battle as the technical and tactical considerations. Therefore, any funds or efforts expanded in the maintenance of security are just as necessary as funds or effort expended in manufacture or development of the project.

2. In order that an absolute control be maintained over the security of the project and that no one individual be allowed to jeopardize the success of the entire undertaking, the following suggested plan is presented:
  A. For an organization that is selected for the project:
   (1) Previous to contact with the project:
    (a) A complete mental and physical examination to be given every member of the organization. Only those individuals who by medical examination can pass a Port of Embarkation examination are to be retained.

Any individuals who are potential limited service, dischargeable for physical disability or liable for a Section VIII proceeding to be transferred from the organization.

(b) A complete examination of the background and previous disciplinary record will be made so that any potentially subversive individuals may also be removed.

(c) A program of security education to be instituted and actually tested.

(d) An officer connected with the project to be attached for control purposes. Many of the problems arising can be solved by reference to previous experiences.

(e) Furloughs to be granted so that all members of the organization may have an opportunity to attend to necessary personal affairs and to maintain morale during the months of training to come.

(2) Upon arrival at school area:

(a) Intense security education to be initiated.

(b) All personnel "frozen"—no transfers from the organization.

(c) Informal censorship to be practiced.

(d) No furloughs to be granted; in cases of dire emergency the minimum time necessary to be granted and the men on furlough will be accompanied by an especially trusted individual of the battalion.

(e) Any man on pass will be accompanied by at least one other member of the battalion.

B. For use throughout the duration of the necessity for secrecy:

(1) The establishment of a Rehabilitation Center consisting of barracks, mess-halls, small hospital and a recreation building.

(2) Men who because of illness or injury require hospitalization.

(3) Men who are placed on limited service.

C. A general policy to be set up as follows:

(1) No man will be released from the Army for any reason. If he is physically or mentally disqualified for general service or limited service be placed in the Rehabilitation Center—to do whatever limited work he can perform. Regulations which require that such persons be discharged should be waived.

(2) Any soldier charged and convicted under the Articles of War and whose sentence is prescribed as confinement will be confined in the Rehabilitation Center and no other place.

(3) If any man goes A.W.O.L.—the immediate cooperation of the F.B.I. to be secured for his immediate return.

CONCLUSION:

All of the above suggestions are based on actual experience with security problems. At present this organization is faced with the difficulty of retaining certain men whose condition normally would mean discharge to civilian life. If these men are sent back to civilian life with the knowledge they now have in their possession, there is no way of adequately assuring secrecy. If these men were to reveal the knowledge they have and the information were to fall into enemy agent's hands, the success of the entire project and all it means would be jeopardized. Admonition, threats or education cannot control a loose tongue under the influence of liquor or prevent a person from inadvertently giving away information he believes innocent. Thus far the Army has spent large sums of money in developing the project. The additional requirements to accomplish the above is believed necessary to assure the complete success of the project.

> STUART L. DANIELS,
> 1st Lieut., 748th Tank Bn (M) (Sp), Adjutant

SOLDIERS' RECOLLECTIONS OF FORT KNOX

First Lt. Daniels' security plan undoubtedly governed the training received by the 736th Tank Battalion (Medium) (Special) and gives a firm context for the memories of training in the oral histories that follow.

The battalion had a couple of weeks at Fort Knox before the special training started. **Pete Henson** recalls what they had to do after their arrival.

In the next couple of days, we had to march nine miles at attention on an orientation hike (probably because we were there under the eyes of the armored force commander). Saw some German tanks and a World War I British tank and marched by the Gold Reserve Vault. I saw lots of military planes flying about, such as P-38, P-39, P-51, P-40, B-25, and Curtiss AT-9's.

When we got back to the barracks, instead of getting to fall out and rest our weary dogs, the colonel made a speech saying, in effect, stay on the ball, no furloughs would be granted, no passes, the outfit was being reorganized, etc.

We started a series of basic training and review exercises, including close order drill and dry runs with the rifle. By the Fourth of July, a lot of men had been busted (demoted); some got labor or stockade for what seemed minor offenses. I was able to avoid most of the unpleasantness by wangling a job in the tool room at the motor pool, under Sgt. Springmeyer, and working with Carson and Pletcher. With all my beer drinking and eating at the PX, I was almost broke for the first time since I got in the army!

Some got weekend passes. Since the majority of the battalion were from Ohio, this made it very nice for them. They lived only three or four hundred miles away. And although they were restricted to a fifty mile radius, no one bothered, at first.

Art Alexander remembers getting home one weekend with his buddy Becket.

We went together. I lived thirty miles from him and I hitch-hiked home and somebody brought me back to his place to come back. He drove.

Gill Terry was another who made it home.

I was able to slip out and hitch-hike my way home, although we were supposed to only go fifty miles, but I went all the way to Cleveland on weekend fifty-mile passes.

Grady Gaston remembers the way guys used to hitch-hike.

I went on one pass with one of my buddies named Carlile, who has been dead a number of years, and went up to visit his mother in Evansville, Indiana. Of course we had to hitchhike up and in those days it was no trouble at all to get a ride if you had on a uniform. You got on a highway and the first person to come along would stop and pick you up and take you as far as they were going and then someone else would come along and take you the distance they were traveling. So it was pretty easy to get around at that time. We enjoyed the weekend at his house and that's the only time I recall being away. And this was before we actually started our training.

For **Joe Perrotti**, the change was sudden.

When I got to Fort Knox, I had spent most of the time at different duties. One morning I got up and somebody says, "Perrotti, your name is on the bulletin board. You've got to be ready to leave." So they told us to get our gear. We were picked up in a GI truck and driven to this place about twenty miles away. This was the place we were enclosed. There was a big fence all around where we were at. There were two ways to get in or out. That's when we were sworn to secrecy. The night before I had been with my brother, who was a military policeman in Kentucky. When he came to get me the next day, the guys told him, "He's gone. We don't know where he went. He got shipped out." No one knew about this camp.

Me and a bunch of guys, we took care of KP at the camp. We used to go to the PX at night and have a few beers. We'd get to watch a movie or something. I wasn't one of the fellows who knew anything about the secret. The guys who were learning weren't talking. At night I'd see these lights up in the sky and I figured it was one of those gas station guys with one of those big things that shoot up in the air for advertising. That's what they were doing. They were startin' to work on this project right there. We had to hurry up because they wanted to use us maybe.

Art Alexander was another in a supporting role at Cedar Creek.

I was one of the guys at STG who wasn't in the tanks. They took me out more or less looking after people. They had a rec *[recreation]* hall there and a place where you had a show and stuff and with me to take care of the place. I'd put ice in the cooler so if there was a show there at night it would keep it cool. It was hot out there. Different things like that. They had other buildings there, like a PX. Some did KP, or other duties to keep things going. You couldn't get in or out. We stayed there three months and couldn't go no place. We took the oath right when we got out to STG. The guys in town didn't know nothin' about it.

Chet Clapper was quite pleased with his assignment at STG.

I was a truck driver. I drove a tank a few times, but only in training. I drove a half-track too. It shifted a little harder than the other vehicles. We pulled trailers with the trucks and had to learn how to back up a trailer on a truck. Truck drivers were Privates or PFCs or T/5's.

I was with Service Company but had to drive a truck out there. I was one that had that secret stuff but I didn't have to go through the classes. I hauled the guys around and stuff like that. I was pretty lucky. The colonel come there one day—I think I was haulin' rocks to make walkways around the buildings. It was way out in the sticks. We was way away from Fort Knox. Most of the tankers were out there. We hauled rocks to make walkways to the eatin' places and the buildings. I imagine a lot of guys trained there afterwards too.

So, the Colonel said, "How'd you like to come and drive jeep for me? I want you to take me over the tank trails."

"OK with me," I told him. Because I was messin' around with them rocks all day in that hot weather, and the rest of the time I just took him out and we was lookin' for tank trails and stuff like that. We was way back in the sticks there one day and we saw a young lady with a baby still feeding on her breast and we talked to her and knew right off the bat talkin' to her that she didn't know nothin' about the war or nothin'. I was surprised and so was the colonel. She had questions. It was so far back in, they had the horse and buggy yet. The mail took a horse and buggy. You get off the main road in Kentucky and Tennessee, years ago, and you're in the sticks.

Bill Sweeney was also a truck driver.

It seemed like all of a sudden it happened and they had this STG group nestled down in a valley between Kentucky hills. I know it was a long hill going down in there and they had governors on the trucks but you could make a game of it. Speed all you could and force or strain the governor without tearing into it. You know how guys are...you'd do anything you could get away with.

Those who didn't get called to the STG had a different time of it. They were able to get into town more often, but had to watch out. Bill Sweeney recalls:

When you went to Louisville, which was a main place for a weekend pass, you'd better be with a buddy. The MP's or whoever knew your outfit, they kept tabs on you. And if you wore your dress cap, the tankers wore it on the left side; all the rest wore it on the right side. They knew who you were and what you were and what you were involved in so you better stick with a buddy.

Clayton Helgeson got in trouble by wearing his dress cap the "proper" tanker way.

We went secret at Fort Knox. We had a fence around the people training on these tanks. We was on the outside. We could go into Louisville. But the guys inside the fence couldn't go anywhere until we got to Camp Bouse. I felt sorry for them guys.

One night we had a buddy pass into Louisville. Major Callison told us "If the MP's ever pick you up, just tell them your name, rank and serial number. You can't tell what outfit you were from or nothin." So we were there in Louisville and it was about two o'clock in the morning and we seen these two girls way up ahead of us about three hundred feet. We was just walkin' along behind them. The MP's stopped us. They checked our pass. Our pass was OK and they wanted to know what outfit we was from. We wasn't allowed to tell them that. All we could tell them was our name, rank and serial number. They thought we was trying to get smart.

First thing, the tankers wear their little caps on the left hand side. That was the side we had it on. We were not drunk or had been drinking. They told us to straighten out our hats and put them on the right side. I said, "No. We wear them on the left side." Then they accused us of being smart. We told them to get ahold of Major Callison at Fort Knox. He'd explain. They took us to the brig there and locked us up.

Major Callison came in later and he wanted to know what we said. I told him exactly what he said: name, rank, and serial number. And they accused us of being smart. So I guess he had a talk with them and said "OK boys, come with me now." So we went back to camp and he interviewed us and found out we didn't do nothin' wrong, so he said "You guys can go back to Louisville."

I said, "Uh, uh. I'm staying right here. I ain't leaving."

We didn't know nothin' about the secret stuff because the tankers was in the stockade there doing their training. I was driving the company jeep. One time they caught us going into Louisville without a pass. The first sergeant, First Sergeant Allen, put us on a twenty-mile march at night. It was rainin'.

For **O.V. Coffman**, also on the outside of the fence, Fort Knox wasn't that great, partly because of the security restrictions.

Then we came to Fort Knox. That's when we went into the CDL's, the Gizmos, went into the training for those. They put us in barracks there at Fort Knox at Seventh and Wilson Road. Some of us they sent out to the school for the Gizmo. Everything was confidential, you couldn't hardly breathe without somebody runnin' down your throat, but after we went out to the school—you didn't get out. But when you did get out, if you got lucky and got to go to town, you went on a five-man buddy pass. If one of them went to the toilet there better be two or three with him. You didn't go by yourself. It was a miserable life. You couldn't go home; you couldn't go on furloughs; hell, you'd have to take five guys with you! How would four other guys want to go home with me? They didn't know none of my family. It was just that simple.

Art Alexander remembers the married guys may have had it easier.

(Francis) Becket wasn't out at STG. He stayed in town. His wife came back with him and stayed there with him. He hung around with Sgt. Hare, who had his wife there too. Their wives hung together. They could go to town together on the buddy pass. His wife was down at Rucker too. A lot of guys had their wives down there. Of course, a lot of us weren't married.

One of those sent to the STG for training was **Grady Gaston**.

I was sent out to this area, restricted area. It was enclosed with a high barbed wire fence so that no one could get in and no one could get out. I believe there were two people from each tank crew, the driver and the special operator. I had the assignment of a special operator at that time. They were teaching us how to operate these tanks with the carbide lights. That was the type of training we did while we was still in Knox. The rest of the company and other parts of the crew were back in the regular base at Fort Knox. I don't know really what they were doing at that time.

The following excerpts from "Pete" Henson's manuscript, "My War," serve as a summary for the adventures at Fort Knox and set the stage for the trip to Bouse, Arizona and the advanced secret training.

A group of men were shipped out but were still carried on the roster. We thought they must be in the field somewhere. We had more restrictions placed on us every day. Our class "A" passes were taken away and we were told we would have to travel in pairs. We got lots of lectures and films on keeping secrets.

At last, at a formation at one of the post theaters, with MPs on the door, we were told about Operation Leaflet, the CDL (Canal Defense Light) and that we had been selected to train in its use.

The reason for traveling in pairs was to keep each other from talking. The CID, G-men, and MP's were on the lookout for any of us caught without their partners, and after five or six men were busted for being alone, we finally realized that they meant business.

I got old "Mort" all cleaned up and sadly, or gladly, turned it in so I was really out of a job. I fired the .30 MG, and then coached on the rifle range for a few days. We finally borrowed four old M-2 halftracks from RTC, and they were really wrecks. Mine, named "Zipper," had 6,600 miles on it, and the cable was showing through the rubber on the tracks. It had old style bogies that I wasn't familiar with. I was assigned to take teams out on the range on it, so they could fire the .30 from a moving vehicle. Once, when coming back from the range on the public highway and driving pretty fast, the left track broke and came off on the pavement. After a short time, I figured out how to make it back to camp without having to wait for maintenance to come and tow us in. We managed to load the track through the back door; it weighed 750 pounds, and by using front wheel drive, I came in on the bogies. It sure looked funny with one track on and the other bogies on the ground.

I started training with the tanks during this period and achieved some fleeting fame by breaking Lt. Gochnour's leg by coming down a hill wide open and running over a log at an angle, so it whipped him around in the commander's hatch and threw him into the .50mg, which was in the stowed position inside the turret. He wore a cast for several weeks. I thought he would be angry, but he just complimented me on my aggressiveness as a tanker and tried to get me to transfer to tanks.

Silas E. Gochnour was a slim, intense man with close-cropped, iron gray hair, from Harrisburg, Pennsylvania. He had been an enlisted man in the peacetime army and had spent some time in the Philippines. During our basic training, he was a stickler for discipline and tried to be something of a martinet. He always spoke in a "parade ground" voice and never just looked or stared at one, but he always glared.

After attending gas warfare school at Edgewood Arsenal, he was appointed gas officer for the battalion and liked nothing better than to catch a group of men relaxing, sneak up, and yell "Gas!" and if anyone was too slow in donning their masks, he would tell them that they were dead.

After the conclusion of basic training, he became more human and, to my surprise, turned out to have a good sense of humor. He would give us lectures on "why we should fight," and one of his favorite expressions was, "You have got to get that urge to kill." He would pick out different ones of the men and tell them because they were Jewish, or Polish, or whatever they were, that they should be glad to fight. When he came to me, I said, "Sir, I'm from Texas. I don't need an excuse to fight." That was the first time I ever saw him crack a smile.

Once, while we were in the field, practicing "cover and concealment," he split the platoon into two sections and sent the first section on ahead to hide and had the other one try to sneak up on them. This was in thick brush, and the first side to see the other was the winner. I found an old foxhole that had some dead limbs over it and, lifting the limbs, crawled in and hunkered down out of sight. I was well hidden and could see several of the men creeping up the hill toward us, and Gochnour himself was coming straight toward me. I stayed hidden, and he passed within five feet of me, looking up the hill trying to spot someone. When he was abreast of my hole, I quietly raised up, poked a stick in his side, and said, "That's all, brother." I didn't know how he would take it, but he was very pleased and called the non-coms over to show them how well I had been concealed.

One day, I drove a 6 x 6 around camp for "Rotten-foot Russell," the supply sergeant. I went to the Quartermaster for some supplies and to the Post Laundry for the company laundry. I always took the longest way around so I could go girl watching. I saw the first WACs here that I had ever seen, including some black girls.

On Friday, July 30, 1943, we found out where all the missing men were when a detail of us were ordered to go to STG (Special Training Group) on Cedar Creek east of the camp, and they were all there. It was a nice little fenced in compound, which most of the boys called "Little Alcatraz," but I really loved it and enjoyed the time there more than any other which I spent at Ft. Knox. We had peace and quiet with no one yelling at us, lots of books, music, and our own theater and PX from which we could start buying beer from 1000 hours on.

There were lots of British officers present—the CDL was a British invention. We had six days of classroom work, and our section had the highest grades in the school, and I was top man in my class. Now we started the practical work. On July 31, 1943, I took my first ride in a "Gizmo," as we called the CDL from then on. We worked 'till midnight and could sleep as late as we wanted—no reveille or roll call to stand. One night, we acted as infantry for a simulated CDL attack and rode in Bren Gun Carriers furnished by the British. They sounded just like a '37 Ford V-8.

Our section consisted of the following: Lt. Gochnour, Cpls. Critchfield, Melendez, and Scarbrough, T-5s Barnes and Henson, PFCs Shoenberger, Crandel, McConnel, Duran, Craytor, and Pvts. Potter, Paarman, Prisel, and Sumter. I volunteered for security patrol on two nights when we patrolled about six and a half miles across the Kentucky hills and forests, which were as black as pitch. Once, we found a grown-over grape vineyard in the dark and filled up on cool, sweet Concord grapes.

Lt. Coveney was acting CO, and while I was on gate guard, he pulled me off and told me of the many advantages of working in maintenance, so I took the job and worked three different shifts in the next two weeks, working on CDL's and old M2A4s, which had been sawed off. I helped pull motors and tracks and even got to test drive them sometimes.

I really liked that little valley, but the PX was so close and so available, I got in the habit of going down for a bottle of "Orange Crush," as the boys called beer, on a moment's notice, or for no notice at all.

While we were there, a practice patrol of the 526th Armored Infantry stumbled into one of our patrols one night, and as they had seen the flashing of the Gizmos on scatter, they were taken into custody and brought to our camp. The upshot of this was a hurried conference of the brass back at Knox, and the entire battalion was attached to us and remained with us till we got overseas. Consequently, they had to go through the censoring and buddy passes like the rest of us. The regular GI's sure hated this situation. My friend, Roger Stiles, from Winslow, Arizona, was in the 526th, and we got to visit a lot before he was killed in Europe.

Our guys back in Knox were going over the hill so badly, and with all the busts and court martials going on, the IG (Inspector General) came around and had a GI bitching session, with the result that he took away the buddy passes (two on a single pass) and reinstated class "A" passes and gave out some five-day furloughs.

When we came back from STG, we were supposed to load right on the train, but plans were changed. We had more "basic training" and lots of road marches. They mistreated us so much that I almost lost my beer belly. Once a section of us went back to Cedar Creek to act as infantry for another outfit. We wore helmets and carried rifles and full field packs. It sure was heavy exercise.

Once, I went into Louisville with Eddie Piper on a buddy pass while they were still in effect. We went to Fountain Ferry Park and rode the rides and chased the girls. We stayed at the Gilbert Hotel, and after we had gone to bed, we heard voices in the next room and saw a light in our bathroom; so upon investigation, discovered a peephole had been drilled in the door, and looking through the hole, saw a beautiful girl undressing. Just as things got interesting, her man, who was standing in the room while this was going on, hung his coat on the bathroom door, cutting off our view. Piper wanted to knock on the door and ask that joker to move his coat. Sunday we took in a couple of movies, drank beer, and got to camp before dark. It became a standing joke at that time to say, "This is it, men! We are going to come off the boat fighting!" because of all the rumors going around.

I, at last, got another halftrack, and as I was now assigned to HQ as a driver, the name had to begin with an "H," so I used "Hombre," which was already painted on it. It had 5,500 miles on it but had been through factory overhaul and was almost like new.

As there was no driving being done, I had to go out on the firing range as a coach while we started qualifying for overseas eligibility. When we told them that they had to shoot a qualifying score or they wouldn't get to go overseas, it was surprising how poorly they shot. I qualified here on the M1917 Revolver as expert with 44 out of 50 in the center ring. I also qualified as expert on the M1911 Automatic. I felt woozy all day and couldn't eat any dinner or supper, so I drank half a gallon of cold milk and as so many of the men were away, I had to walk guard all night, and the next day I was really sick. The humidity was approaching 100 percent, and even though the temperature was only in the high eighties, I almost passed out.

We lay around on alert from August 18, 1943 till September 4, 1943. The officers and non-coms had to keep us busy and seemed to be afraid we would have a moment's peace. Lt. Coveney and Sgt. McCarthy took us on a full field hike on the hottest day of the year. Several guys fell out on Agony Hill and Misery Mountain, and I thought I was about gone myself. I stopped to aid Corporal Yokum, who had passed out, and had to double-time 200 yards to catch up. Not knowing ahead of time about this march, I had a new pair of shoes on, and when we returned, my feet were a solid blister. That's the hottest I have been in my entire life.

After all the demonstrations were over at Hays School (STG), I got Saturday off and a pass to go with Herston Hogue to his home at Waynesburg, Kentucky. We rode the bus part way and hitchhiked the rest. We brought a shoe box with us that had two pints of "Old Tanglefoot" in it. We got Mr. Hogue's 1939 Chevy and went out "amongst–em" Saturday night. Went to church on Sunday and walked Vernelle, Hogue's sister, home, ate a big Sunday dinner and went over to see Granny, 102 years old and still living alone.

Hitchhiking back to Danville, we met two real hillbilly girls named Dora Lee and, so help me, Gerty Lou at the bus station and rode back to Louisville with them. They were a barrel of laughs. It was a very fine weekend.

They laid on a trip to Mammoth Cave for us, and I got to drive on it. I was always ready to drive anything. We toured the cave, hiking four miles underground and took a boat ride 300 feet under ground.

At last, on September 4, 1943, we got orders to load on the train. We sat around on our musette bags most of the morning, waiting for the Pullmans to be spotted. We spent our time watching the girls through our binoculars and playing an old guitar belonging to Dale Cork.

Organized outing for Company "A" to Mammoth Cave, Kentucky on Sunday, August 8, 1943.
(photo thanks to Martin Depoian and Wayne Foote)

CHAPTER 6

The California-Arizona Maneuver Area and Brief History of the 150th Station Hospital while at Camp Bouse, Arizona

Part A. The California-Arizona Maneuver Area
Introduction

The Desert Training Center was a vast area covering more than 10,000 square miles. In the spring of 1943 it was made even larger with the addition of another 7,700 square miles on the eastern side of the Colorado River, designated as "Area B" and "Area C." Major General Charles H. White, as commander of IX Corps, assumed responsibility for operating the Desert Training Center on 29 March 1943, and the expansion occurred on his watch. The DTC was now an area larger than the state of Pennsylvania. The name of the Center was also changed to the California-Arizona Maneuver Area (CAMA). The definitive history of the Desert Training Center and CAMA, Study No. 15, was compiled by Sgt. Sidney L. Meller after the war in 1946. He wrote:

> The name of the Center was changed. Not a precursor of things to come, this was rather a public acknowledgement of the modification in purpose that had taken place in late 1942 and early 1943. The name of the Desert Training Center had aroused the question of why training in a desert should be continued when no further prospect of using our army in desert terrain remained. The question missed the real issue, since the Army Ground Forces wished to continue operations in the desert because of its desirability as a general training area. The Desert Training Center, by an order effective 20 October 1943, became the California-Arizona Maneuver Area.

This chapter includes two documents which serve as an overview for the experience at Camp Bouse. The first is an excellent description of the California-Arizona Maneuver Area, where the battalions were sent to train after they left Fort Knox. We found this contemporary account in the National Archives. Captain Herbert Chase, MI (Military Intelligence), compiled the document in his role as the Public Relations Officer of CAMA. The information, issued at Camp Young Headquarters, California on 19 November 1943, portrays the sheer size of the undertaking, its geographic spread and importance for military training. Of course, there is no mention of the secret training at Camp Bouse.

HEADQUARTERS
CALIFORNIA-ARIZONA MANEUVER AREA
Camp Young, California
19 November 1943
CALIFORNIA-ARIZONA MANEUVER AREA

I
GENERAL

The California-Arizona Maneuver Area is a Training Theatre of Operations covering an area 550 miles long and 250 miles wide extending from Pomona, California, on the West, to Phoenix, Arizona, on the East; and from Yuma, Arizona, on the South, to Boulder City, Nevada, on the North. This area is divided into a Combat Zone and a Communications Zone. The Combat Zone occupies approximately the eastern two-thirds of this area and the Communications Zone comprises the western third.The Headquarters of California-Arizona Maneuver Area is located at Camp Young, California, 26 miles east of Indio.

The Headquarters of the Communications Zone is at San Bernardino, California. The mission of the California-Arizona Maneuver Area is to train, maintain, and supply troops realistically as in a Theatre of Operations. The training is designed to harden troops physically and to train soldiers mentally for the shock of battle. Much of the firing is conducted under realistic battle conditions. Other objectives are the development of tactics, techniques, and training methods suitable for desert warfare, and to test and develop equipment and supplies.

II

The terrain of the combat zone varies from a series of dry lakes and sandy valleys to high and rugged mountains. Elevation ranges from 240 feet below sea level at the surface of the Salton Sea, a large salt lake on the boundary between the Combat Zone and the Communications Zone, to 7,400 feet at the top of some of the mountain ranges. This is the only lake, and there is only one river, the Colorado, which flows across the area generally from north to south.

Some areas are covered with fine sand and have little or no vegetation. Other areas are surfaced with hard gravel-like stretches known as "desert pavements," caused by rain washing loose sand through the hard gravel. The latter is merely an outside crust which, if broken, exposes the soft material underneath. In certain sections large sand dunes, sometimes 40 feet high, are formed by the wind.

The principal obstacles to free maneuvers are two railroad lines and the Los Angeles Metropolitan Aqueduct, running east and west, and the mountain ranges, most of which run north and south. Military vehicles may cross the railroad and aqueduct only at designated places. The mountains may be by-passed although many of the passes are narrow and permit only limited movement. Sand dunes between Granite Mountain and the Colorado River and in the area west of Yuma are virtually impassable. The Colorado River is another major barrier, 800 feet wide in places, and has a swift current with whirlpools, sandbars, and rapidly changing bed foundations which make bridge operations and swimming dangerous.

California-Arizona Maneuver Area is the largest Army training center in the United States and probably in the world, covering an area considerably larger than England. The Combat Zone alone is 20% larger than Switzerland, and is extremely arid and sparsely populated. There are less than 10 cities and towns ranging in population from 125 at Desert Center to less than 5,000 in Yuma. When General Patton was on a reconnaissance trip preparing a report on this territory for the Secretary of War, his party traveled four days without seeing an inhabitant.

The rigors of the area provide excellent training for drivers and maintenance personnel. Here, due to the heat, dust, and the difficult terrain over which vehicles must operate, an overhaul is required after each 3,000 miles. Under normal conditions elsewhere vehicles travel 10,000 miles before requiring this service.

Water supply in the maneuver area is obtained from six sources: the Colorado River, the Metropolitan Aqueduct, irrigation canal systems, the larger municipal supplies, railroad wells, and various other springs and wells. Approved water sources are designated as Water Points, and no water is used from any questionable well, spring, or other unauthorized source.

One unacquainted with the area is surprised by its clear air and the resulting exaggerated detail which makes distant objects look nearer. It is not uncommon to see a mountain 75 miles away so clearly that it seems to be no more than 15 or 20 miles distant.

The lack of natural concealment in the area places special emphasis on camouflage. Shadow movements are the principal source of information as to the location and nature of objects, and every effort must be made to conceal or distort them, and to reduce them by digging in vehicles and weapons. Maximum use should be made of natural shadows in broken ground, dry washes, and sand dune areas.

The climate of the area is dry. In the warmest periods the temperature may rise as high as 125°. The greatest problem is not in the extreme heat, but rather in the large variation in daily temperature. In the summer the temperature frequently drops from over 100° in the day to under 75° at night, and in the winter the temperature may change from freezing in the early morning to as high as 100° at mid-day. Sudden changes frequently take place without warning. A cloudburst, wind storm or sudden change in temperature may occur at any time. Yearly rainfall is less than five inches. The prevailing winds are from the south in summer and from the north in winter. July, August, and September are the rainy months. Troops are warned against bivouacking at night in draws or washes. There are numerous plants native to the desert which thrive in heat and dryness. The principal types are cacti, greasewood or creosote plant, sagebrush and occasional Joshua Trees. A few palms are found in clumps near water. Other types of plants are the Spanish bayonet, the ocotillo, Snake Trees, and Palo Verde Guayule, a rubber-bearing weed. There are some 250 species of plants native to this area.

There are centipedes, scorpions, tarantulas, and Black Widow spiders. Bites are painful and dangerous. There are several species of rattlesnakes. The one most prevalent is the small horned side-winder. There is also found one type of coral snake.

The climate of the California-Arizona Maneuver Area is healthful and sickness from disease is rare. Much of the freedom from disease is due to the vigilance with which fly-control and water purification measures are applied. Troops in the area are living under field conditions. The only sanitary provisions are the simple field sanitary installations.

III
HISTORY

In March 1942, when it appeared that the African Campaign would play a major role in the war, plans were made for giving our troops desert training. General George S. Patton, Commanding General of the 1st Armored Corps, was designated to organize and command which was then known as the Desert Training Center. He used his 1st Armored Corps Staff, augmented by certain personnel detailed from Army Ground Forces. At first the headquarters was in Indio. During the month of April about 10,000 troops arrived. These were non-divisional units including Tanks, Tank Destroyers, Artillery, Anti-Aircraft, Engineer, Medical, Truck, and other units, mostly separate regiments, battalions, and companies.

This location was designated as Camp Young, in May 1942, and all troops in Desert Training Center were stationed here. These were used as development troops for the study of desert tactics and technique. Extensive reconnaissance of the desert was made using army vehicles and liaison-type planes.

The 2nd Armored Corps, commanded by General Gillem, followed the 1st at Desert Training Center. While they were here, the first large maneuvers were conducted. Participating in these maneuvers, among other units, was the VII Army Corps commanded by General Richardson. Then came the IV Armored Corps commanded by General Walker, and the IX Army Corps under command of General White, then the XV Army Corps under Maj. Gen. Haislip.

In 1943 the Communications Zone was established with headquarters at San Bernardino. A Base General Depot was organized at San Bernardino also, an Ordnance Depot at Pomona, and an Ammunition Depot at Fontana. Replacement Depots were organized, Station Hospitals established, and Advance Railheads set up.

During the past year and a half California-Arizona Maneuver Area has grown to its present size, covering portions of California, Arizona, and Nevada, and training simultaneously almost 200,000 troops under the command of Major General Alexander M. Patch, Jr, and his IV Corps Staff.

HERBERT CHASE
Captain MI
Public Relations Officer

Part B. An overview of life at Camp Bouse from the official history of the 150th Station Hospital: 31 August 1943–27 April 1944

The second document also comes from the National Archives. While researching the story of the 736th Tank Battalion, we came across the official history of a support unit crucial to maintaining the training effort—the 150th Station Hospital. Since it was one of the first units to arrive and virtually the last to leave, the document has a valuable place in our story. The author is unknown. This document is a sometimes frank and often revealing account of the experiences at Camp Bouse. The narrative, not written in military jargon, provides an overview for the other documents and stories of the 736th Tank Battalion which comprise the rest of the chapter. One of the nurses in the hospital unit, Mrs. Josephine Macpherson, has kindly provided photographs of the camp which were taken in 1943.

The 150th (US) Station Hospital was activated in 1943 and began its history at Camp Wheeler, Georgia. There the members went through their basic training and the enlisted personnel attended schools and assisted in the Station Hospital of Camp Wheeler in order to qualify as technicians with the 150th. During this time the unit furnished personnel for three ships' platoons.

Then, at the end of August 1943, the 150th Station Hospital, now attached to the 9th Tank Group, arrived at Camp Bouse, Arizona and began operations under the same kinds of restrictions as faced the other units. The requirements for secrecy were such that the medical personnel had to take care of all manner of injuries and illnesses, psychological as well as physical, since no one could be transferred out of the camp for treatment.

The 150th Station Hospital

On 31 August 1943, the 150th Station Hospital began operations in an isolated desert area of Arizona assigned to a secret project. During the latter part of 1943, the organization adjusted itself to the initial difficulties of heat, water shortage, and the maintenance of security. There was an extreme minimum of evacuation of patients so that definitive care was performed whenever possible.

This fifty-bed station hospital was assigned to the Ninth Service Command but attached and under the control of the Army Ground Force and Armored Command for the purpose of serving some 5,600 troops who were training in this secret project. The site of the camp had been chosen with one eye to secrecy and isolation and the other to a topography suitable to the nature of the project, both factors being unfavorable to a hospital.

The camp adopted the name of the nearest railhead, hence was called Camp Bouse, although officially it was merely an APO number, a blank unrecorded space on the map. There were armed guards at the two mountain passes leading into the valley, and the high mountains served as a further barrier. Although located within the United States, the camp was on a quasi-foreign soil status, for all outgoing mail was censored, and enlisted men could only go out on "buddy passes" in groups of five (and later two or three) when an occasional recreational convoy took the men into a town large enough to stand the influx of a truckload or two of soldiers—seventy-five miles away. These passes required that the five men remain in the presence of each other—in a theatre, in a bar, in a latrine—and even on furloughs a companion had to be taken along. The hospital was as thoroughly enmeshed by the secret as were the active participants, the battalions, the project creating a tightly closed group from which no one could get out. Transfers outside the project were prohibited; attendance to service schools was forbidden; discharges were impossible.

Those men who merited discharge for medical reasons had to be retained in service, as the authorities ambiguously put it, "until such time as the military situation permits." In one unusual case, an enlisted man had been discharged from service from an outside general hospital in which he had been hospitalized while on pass or furlough, and orders were sent to his local draft board to redraft him immediately in order that he remain part of the project. Evacuation of patients along ordinary channels was impossible, and there were only three general hospitals to which patients could be sent in extreme cases, and even then they were kept in isolated wards incommunicado from ordinary patients.

There were two small buildings for wards—one for the more serious medical cases, the other for surgical cases—and as the camp grew, the rest of the patients lived in ward and pyramidal tents. The only cement walk in the entire camp was a short stretch of about twenty yards between the clinic building and the mess hall, which were practically the only other buildings in an otherwise tented camp, for all troops and battalion headquarters were quartered in pyramidal tents.

As more troops came into the project, the water supply had to be improved by augmenting it with a large water tower of wood which allowed occasional showers from pipes instead of from steel helmets.

On 7 January 1944, a directive from the Secretary of War to the Commanding General, Ninth Service Command, the Surgeon General, and Chiefs of Technical Services, ASF, ordered the reorganization of the 150th Station Hospital (50-bed) to a 150-bed unit. The directive, calling for immediate action by 10 January, authorized a doubling of staff to accommodate a tripling in size of the facility. Officers increased from 7 to 13, nurses from 6 to 15 and enlisted men from 41 to 97. Without exception, personnel already assigned to the unit would be retained after reorganization. The Surgeon General had authorization to increase staff without needing a requisition.

Effective 20 January 1944, the unit was relieved from assignment to the Ninth Service Command, attachment to the Army Ground Forces, and the Armored Command, and placed under the control of the Commanding General, Army Ground Forces and reassigned to the Armored Command. Then on 30 January 1944, orders were cut by the Headquarters, Ninth Armored Group, relieving the unit from attachment and attaching it to Headquarters, 10th Armored Group, "same station."

This became a turbulent time for all the units at Bouse as they made preparations for departure to Europe while still completing required training assignments. The record of the 150th Station Hospital, now three times the size of the original Camp Bouse unit, eloquently understates the feelings during the time of transition.

January. On 10 January 1944, the 150th Station Hospital was reorganized from a fifty-bed unit to one hundred fifty beds, and concomitant with the reorganization, came the authority to increase the personnel from seven officers to thirteen, from six nurses to twelve, from forty-two enlisted men to ninety-seven. About the same time, the hospital was reassigned to Armored Command. Officers, nurses, and even wardmen were the butt of numerous queries concerning the triangular patch of Armored Command that they, as medical personnel, were wearing.

Numerous promotions of technicians to appropriate grades were made under the new Table of Organization. Seven new officers were assigned to the hospital in January. Because of ill health [one captain] was transferred to Nichols General Hospital, never to report to the organization for duty again.

Swelling the ranks of enlisted personnel were new transfers from almost everywhere. This influx gave us an over-strength in grade of enlisted men due to the non-commissioned officers of higher grades who had been sent in, a fact which played havoc with the existing table of organization, but as the dim of secrecy blocked up all normal outlets and transfers, there was dammed up into a stagnant pool of overage in grade....

As the tactical units began moving overseas, scores of men were boarded by the hospital's Disposition Board, and were reclassified as unfit for combat duty, and soon the hospital was boarding enlisted men whom the battalions did not want because of either voluntary or involuntary characteristics of the men themselves. "Salt water fever" even infected some of the officers, too.

February. Our adjutant was sick while on leave, and it was only due to the magic of penicillin that he was saved from an infection around his eye. A young roentgenologlst was transferred into the hospital. [He was] still damp with the veneer of a medical school degree and the subsequent coating of Army Roentgenological School training. Still another officer was lost to the hospital when [another captain] was transferred as a patient to Torney General Hospital, Palm Springs, California.

March. March winds blew up more than blinding clouds of sand, for the cauldron of officer personnel was still bubbling due perhaps to heat stirred up by the coals of alerts of various units, and advance notices sent to the hospital. The fact that Camp Bouse was beginning to break up was more tangible when one of our officers had to escort several battalions to a staging area and soon thereafter three of our officers were reclassified at Torney General Hospital as permanent limited service. In all fairness, it might be added that this was a protective measure rather than a subterfuge, for the hospital, being under Armored Command, was completely at the mercy of the Armored Groups who, playing lord and master, transferred officers and enlisted men into and out of the hospital and Battalions as if the personnel concerned were all pieces, however differently shaped, on a chess board. One of the battalions moving out took one of our general service officers, (and gave us an ailing officer of their own).

Unofficially, we knew at this time that the hospital, too, would soon be alerted, and pre-overseas physicals were held among the men of the hospital detachment, weeding out those who would not pass the physical at the Port of Embarkation. Those in the hospital detachment and in the battalions who were completely unfit for overseas duty, but who couldn't be discharged, having been indoctrinated with the secret, were transferred into a bastard unit known first as Provisional Overhead Company and later as STG, Special Training Group, which consisted of the dregs from all units in the project. This unit performed such tasks as running the Post Exchange, Post Office, and was slated to be the clean-up detail at Camp Bouse after the others had gone. Six of the hospital's officers were transferred to Special Training Group, including the captain with the ailing kidneys, but we received two of the six back into the hospital to fill up a waning Table of Organization when, after much discussion, it was seen that officer personnel could be sent overseas with the hospital despite classification as limited service. Security was relaxed enough to allow the men to take pre-overseas furloughs without having to cross the threshold of their homes with a desert mate to guard their speech.

April. The month of April, [in] the latter part of which we finally moved out of the desert, was characterized by an increasing crescendo of activities. Show-down inspections, physical fitness tests, packing, crating, last minute transfers, and the ultimate farewell to the desert. The hospital finally transferred an enlisted man whose talents lay in becoming constantly involved in court-martial offenses. To make up losses of enlisted personnel and build enlisted strength up to the authorized Table of Organization amount plus five percent over-strength the Armored Groups were kind enough to dip into their stagnant pool of Special Training Group, which it will be remembered received the unwanted and unfit-for-combat men from the battalions, and pulled out tank drivers, armorers, and motor mechanics as replacements for the skilled medical technicians that the hospital could not take overseas because of physical defects. In other words, the enlisted men that the battalions did not want were offered to the hospital, for "anyone can be a medic," they said.

Meanwhile the hospital disposition board was working violently to try to digest the large lumps of allegedly unfit men that the battalions kept pushing at them as they started to leave the desert one by one. Some of the same men were seen several times, thanks to the mismanagement of the Armored Group by which the reports of the dispositions would disappear within a matter of hours after they were placed in their message center. Each battalion commander felt justified in his attempt to bring pressure upon the hospital to (1) reclassify large numbers of men within two or three days and (2) reclassify them the way they wanted them to be reclassified regardless of medical opinion.

One of the enlisted men, the assistant laboratory technician, had applied for a commission in the Sanitary Corps long before he had joined the secret project, and two weeks before the hospital left the desert, his commission came through, much to his surprise and to the consternation of project authorities, for the transfer of personnel was supposed to be forbidden, all personnel being frozen. No position was open for [him] in the hospital, and as his orders came from Washington, D. C., nothing much could be done about them even though Washington had previously said that no one could or would get out of the secret. In this one instance, however, the bewildered young man finally succeeded in getting out of the project after being lectured to and impressed with his unique status as the first and only person to get out.

One of the main problems encountered was that of packing and disposing of the supplies. Eight months of hospital accumulations had to be boxed with scrap lumber, and disposed of, for the hospital was to travel "4k" according to Preparation for Overseas Movement instructions, with only a minimum of records and equipment. The California-Arizona maneuver area was closing up, as were numerous camps and depots in the desert area, and a major headache was trying to find a place to ship the hospital equipment. The hospital continued to operate as such until the last week or so, even during the time that equipment was being boxed and packed. As the battalions left, the carpenter even had to make trips into the deserted battalion areas to salvage wood for packing from the empty tent frames. The camp was a skeleton of itself, with tents that had somehow given an impression of solidity after the many months disappearing overnight. It was like that at the hospital, too, an unbelievable disintegration that one had to accept.

The advance detachment of the 150th Station Hospital moved out—three officers and two enlisted men. These men were to report to Fort Knox, Kentucky, and then precede the hospital to its overseas location. The main body of the hospital was to follow to Fort Knox, where it would pick up clothing and equipment which was unobtainable due to the inactivation of supply depots in the desert area. On 27 April 1944, the 150th Station Hospital personnel rode over the bumpy dusty road that led out to civilization for the last time, boarded a long troop train, shook the sand of Camp Bouse from its clothes for the final time, and departed for Fort Knox, Kentucky, which was to be a preliminary staging area.

The hospital—Clinic building, Admissions tent, Surgical ward

Left to Right: Josephine Sokolowski, Ruth Lupo, Lois Fisher
[note tents in background]

Left to Right: 2nd Lts. Lorene Jackson, Ruth Lupo, Lois Fisher,
Ruth Nations, Josephine Sokolowski

The nurses' quarters

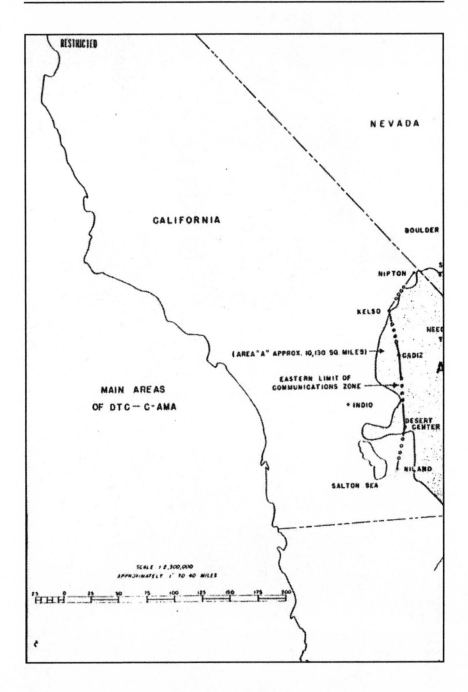

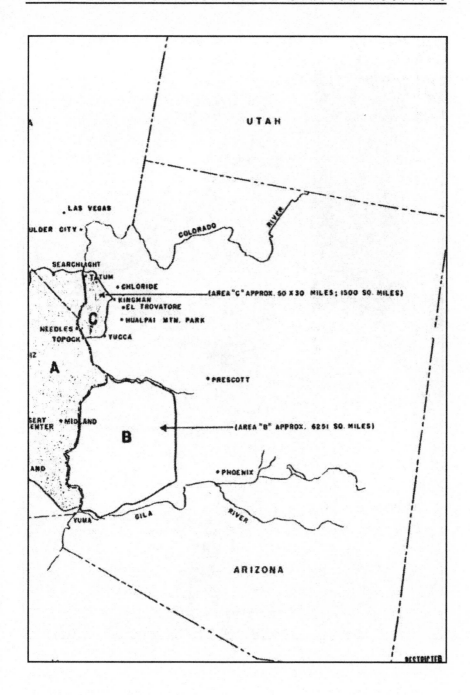

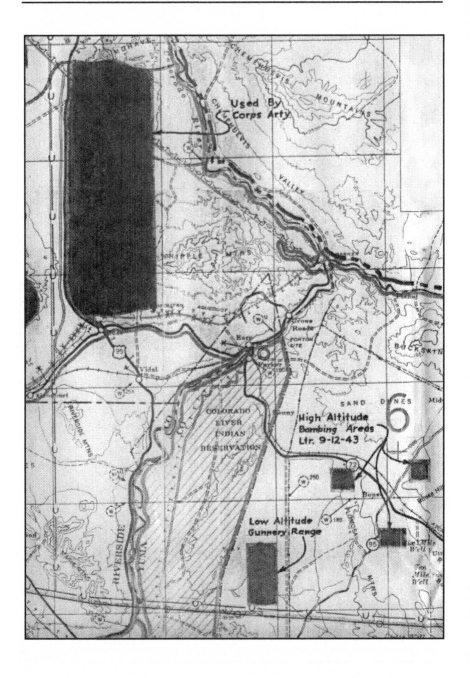

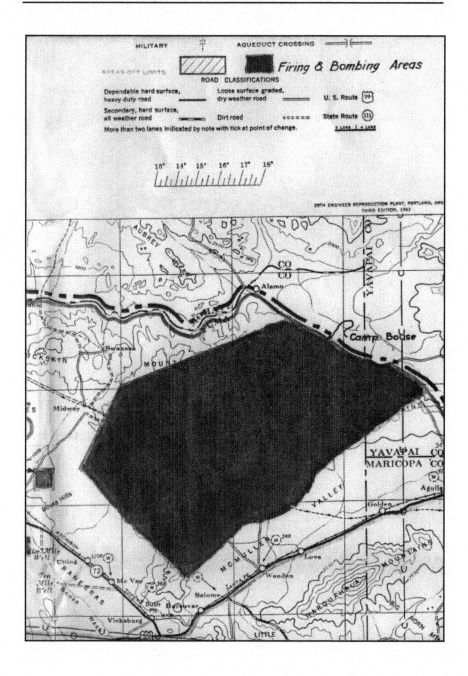

CHAPTER 7

Secret Battle Training at Camp Bouse, Arizona

Introduction

At Fort Knox, the secret training was limited to familiarization with operation of the light. This involved the driver, operator and assistant driver. The instructors had a wire cage built on the back outside the turret. From there they would instruct the crew by radio and communicate as well with the other tanks on the other runways. [Carsie Denning, personal communication.] But this was not battle training. For that they needed a much larger area in which to simulate combat conditions. They chose "Area B" of the Desert Training Center in Arizona.

Once the Army decided where the follow-on secret training would take place, Lt. Col. Joseph H. Gilbreth, Lt. Col. George K. Rubel, Executive Officer, and two other officers from the Ninth Tank Group were transferred to Camp Young, Desert Training Center. The transfer took place on July 11. The advanced party of the 748th Tank Battalion followed them. The 748th Tank Battalion itself departed Fort Knox on 15 July, and bivouacked for the next five weeks in the Desert Training Center on the California side of the Colorado River. They were about one hundred and twenty five miles from their final destination, waiting for orders to move to Camp Bouse. ("Saga of the Rhinos," n.d.)

On 17 August, the Headquarters and Headquarters Detachment of the 9th Tank Group departed Camp Campbell, Kentucky, at 0925 and moved by rail to the Desert Training Center. They arrived in Bouse, Arizona, 20 August at 2300 and "began building a semi-permanent camp for special training." The entry in the (S-2)-(S-3) Journal for the following day is understated in its simplicity: "Aug. 21, 1943—Usual camp duties." (Notes on Unit History, Headquarters Ninth Armored Group, 19 September 1945, National Archives.)

Meanwhile, court actions were securing the area in Butler Valley for the secret operations. On 12 August, an "Order for Immediate Possession" was filed in the U.S. District Court for the District of Arizona. Some eighty-three respondents, including nine mining companies, as well as all "unknown owners and claimants" of lands in the desired area, were barred from their lands "by condemnation under judicial process." Through this action, the United States took immediate possession of all the lands specified and funds were appropriated for payment of just compensation.

The court order did not finish the matter. The National Archives documents include an interesting record of an important telephone conversation on the topic made on 6 September at 1045 by Lt. Col. Gilbreth:

> Colonel Hawkins (Housing and Training Aids Branch,
> Army Ground Forces, Washington D.C.) stated he
> would contact Colonel Ennis and call me back.
> I informed him of the situation reference miners in
> the valley and stated definitely that the operations
> of the two designated mines would interfere with the
> operations of the 9th Tank Group. It appears to be a
> political aspect. It is to be referred to the planning
> personnel, Army Ground Forces, for decision.

Meanwhile, efforts continued at Camp Bouse to control the miners. On October 5, Major Warten and Captain Fritsvold reached a temporary accommodation with them. The two miners had signed an agreement that they would abide by four specific regulations. First, they would hire no one whose loyalty had not been investigated by the military authorities. Second, they would hire no one who had been found disloyal. Third, they would comply with existing camp regulations regarding passes, and fourth, they would clear all personnel from within the camp boundaries from sunset to sunrise.

But the Army was not in a mood to tolerate this sort of civilian presence in the valley. Major Hughes, S2, Hq 9th Tank Group sent off a telegram transmitted by the Signal Corps to the Commanding General, Armored Command, at Fort Knox, with attention Major L. A. Martin:

LELANDER INFORMS LATEST ADVICES WASHINGTON MINERS WILL NOT REPEAT NOT OPERATE IN VALLEY STOP INCIDENT CONSIDERED CLOSED

A copy of this telegram was sent Col. Gilbreth by Brigadier General John L. Pierce, G.S.C., Chief of Staff, on 22 October. So the miners quit their operations in the valley, but they abandoned one of their hard-working creatures, a donkey. The donkey adopted the camp and became pet and mascot until Christmas Eve, when he met his demise. We conclude the oral history interviews in Chapter Eight with the story of "8-Ball."

Units begin arriving at Camp Bouse, DTC
On 30 August, the 736th Tank Battalion (M) (Sp) received orders attaching it to the 9th Tank Group once it reached the Desert Training Center.

R E S T R I C T E D

HEADQUARTERS ARMORED COMMAND
Fort Knox, Kentucky

30 August 1943.

GENERAL ORDERS)
           :
NUMBER 81)

       I. RELIEF FROM ATTACHMENT OF 740TH TANK BATTALION (M).
      II. ATTACHMENT OF 92ND MACHINE RECORDS UNIT.
     III. ATTACHMENT OF UNITS TO 9TH TANK GROUP.

   I.   The 740th Tank Battalion (M), Fort Knox, Kentucky, is relieved
from attachment to Headquarters and Headquarters Detachment, 8th Tank
Group, same station, effective 8 September 1943.

   II. The 92nd Machine Records Unit, Fort Knox, Kentucky, is attached
to Headquarters Company, Armored Command, same station, for quarters and
rations only, effective 1 September 1943.

   III. The following units are relieved from previous attachments and
are attached to 9th Tank Group, Desert Training Center on the dates indicated.

UNIT	DATE
748th Tank Battalion (M)(Sp)	30 August 1943
736th Tank Battalion (M)(Sp)	Upon arrival at DTC
538th Ordnance Heavy Maintenance Company (Tk)	Upon arrival at DTC
526th Armored Infantry Battalion	Upon arrival at DTC
150th Station Hospital	Upon arrival at DTC

       By command of Major General GILLEM:

                                   JOHN L. PIERCE,
                                   Brigadier General, G.S.C.,
                                   Chief of Staff.

OFFICIAL:

RAYMOND STONE JR
COL AGD
AG

DISTRIBUTION "D".

R E S T R I C T E D

As the soldiers selected for the secret training were making their way to Camp Bouse, Lt. Col. Rubel, was overseeing the installation of camp infrastructure. On 13 September he phoned Fort Knox with an update. This is such an interesting and informative document that we include it here. Lt. Col. Rubel begins with a discussion of the water situation, then briefs on progress in setting up the hospital, tank park, school building and ammunition magazine. He mentions the road-building activity and issues with the generator and fire-fighting apparatus. He also has questions about the Table of Organization for the 526th Armored Infantry Battalion and makes a request that the engineer company from the 20th Armored Division remain until the end of October. Here is a summary of some of the key points in the transcribed telephone conversation:

- **Water supply**. The water pump was started. A 500,000 gallon storage tank was excavated, but no concrete had been poured. A booster was on hand for the water system to boost it into the tank tower, but it wasn't installed yet. The chlorinator to chlorinate water was on hand but not yet installed. "We have the wrong type of chlorine cylinder. Probably take couple of weeks to get right kind. The water tower is wooden. It has been erected, but it will not hold water. Someone from DTC will be down soon and try to do something about it."

- **Structures**. Surgical and clinical building has the roof up. The inside is still incomplete. Probably will be a week before it is ready to occupy. Surgical ward building has floor finished and part of the walls up. They are just beginning to put the floor together in the medical ward.

- Shop building in tank park area is partly framed. They claim they have no framing material to finish this…. School building is partly framed. Part of the roof is up. No work done inside yet….

- Special equipment. Most importantly, we note Colonel Rubel's request for an update about "special equipment," i.e., the leaflets.

HEADQUARTERS ARMORED FORCE
Fort Knox, Kentucky

Record of Important
Telephone Conversation

This form will be used whenever a staff officer gives a decision or receives information over the telephone on which action affecting this Headquarters is to be based or where a new policy or change in existing policy is enunciated or contemplated. This record will be made immediately after the conversation.

Person Calling __Lt. Col. Rubel__   Place __Camp Bouse, Arizona__

Official Position __Executive Officer, 9th Tank Group__

Person Called __Lt. Col. Malaga__   Place __Fort Knox, Kentucky__

Official Position __Assistant G-3, Armd Comd__

Date __13 September 1943__   Time __1100__

Synopsis of Conversation:

The following information was given by Col. Rubel:

The operation of the water pump was started today. 500,000 gallon storage tank is excavated, but no concrete has been poured. We have a booster for the water system to boost it into the tank tower, but it is not installed. Will probably be installed within two or three days. We have a chlorinator to chlorinate water, but it is not installed. Will probably be installed within next two or three days. We have wrong type of chlorine cylinder. Probably take couple of weeks to get right kind. The water tower is wooden. It has been erected, but it will not hold water. Someone from DTC will be down soon and try to do something about it.

About the buildings:

Surgical and clinical building has the roof up. The inside is still incomplete. Probably will be a week before it is ready to occupy.

Surgical ward building has floor finished, and part of the walls up. Week or ten days at very least on that. Probably two to three weeks actually.

They are just beginning to put the floor together in the medical ward.

Just finishing concrete forms for foundation of patients' mess building.

Shop building in tank park area is partly framed. They claim they have no framing material to finish this. I will find out later in the week when they expect to get it.

‾‾‾‾‾‾‾‾‾‾‾‾‾‾‾‾‾‾‾‾
(Signature)

1 Copy to Chief of Staff for Information
1 Copy to Adjutant General for file.
C/S, AG, G-1, G-4, G-3, Sig Off
Given col muller for file B.R.R. 80843

School building is partly framed. Part of the roof is up. No work done inside yet.

Repair building, maintenance shop (smaller of two large buildings) has not been started yet. They are beginning to make up some forms for the foundation.

No work yet on ammunition magazine out in the area to store ammunition. They are still talking about plans to build it. Communications Zone is charged with this work. In the meantime, we have two carloads of ammunition on the ground. We have tents over it. Another carload of ammunition is on the way.

Roads in and out of the camp are incomplete. They say anywhere from one month to two or three months work on the roads.

The generator that starts the engine has burned out. We are borrowing a welder at night. It is temporary hook-up only. The electrical system throughout the camp is very incomplete. Will be completed in a week or ten days at the very least. That generator has been sent away for re-winding. It will work, but will not be sufficient to operate the entire camp. The one we have now is being used by engineers to run pipe-threading machine, so we cannot operate our TWX. Will have TWX operating within a week.

Both electrical generators are in the same building. That is quite a fire hazard. All we need to remedy the situation is a small building. I think that is very advisable. The generators are diesel-driven. They have electrical system on the engine to start it. I recommend strongly that we get another building. Then we could put one plant in each building.

We are having considerable difficulty getting fire-fighting apparatus. We are having considerable difficulty getting all supplies except rations and fuel. We requested fire-fighting equipment, but DTC turned it down saying they didn't think it was necessary. We have had two fires here already. Both were in the Engineer Camp - one burned up the power saw in the carpenter shop, and the other burned the generator. We are told that we have no status as a camp - we are only a bivouac. Anything not TBA, such as fire-fighting equipment, is Post, Camp and Station property, and as a bivouac we are not entitled to it. (NOTE: Recommend we request AGF to authorize an additional building to house the second generator and authorize fire-fighting apparatus.)

We requested DTC to make some aerial photographs of Butler Valley. They do not have any equipment to do the job. However, the 6th Engineer Photographic Group at Denver, under AGF control, is the nearest unit. They are available, and can do the job, provided we go through AGF. Will send in letter on this.

Under what T/O should the 526th Armored Infantry Battalion operate? We need this information in order to draw vehicles from DTC. DTC is all right on every-thing except this Post, Camp and Station supply business. They have been co-operating in a fine manner.

- 2 -

Request that the engineer company from the 20th Armored Division remain until 31 October. Reason: to finish building roads, and when we close the gates, they can finish the road from the gates to the railhead, about 10 miles away. They do not have the necessary equipment, but if they can stay, we can get the equipment. The 369th Engineers, who are building the camp now, expect to go on maneuvers not later than 28 September, regardless of whether the camp is complete. However, if they go, the 220th can finish the job.
(NOTE: Recommend we ask AGF for authority to keep the Engineer Company from 20th Armd Div until 31 October.)

We need the three SCR-506 radios, 12 volt, authorized for Hq & Hq Det, 9th Tank Group, for our security measures.

General Pierce said he would authorize between 70 and 100 additional men for the detachment. We need those men as soon as possible - it is all right if they come in driblets. Ship men to Bouse, Arizona.

Telegraph address: Bouse, Arizona.

538th Ordnance Company arrived at 2 AM this morning.

Is there any such thing as G-3 funds for training aids? (Will send in letter on this.)

Is there any special equipment ready for shipment? (Col. Rubel was told that they would be notified when equipment is available.)

R. J. HALADA,
Lt Col, Infantry,
Assistant G-3.

By mid-September, two tank battalions, an armored infantry battalion, an ordnance company and the hospital unit were settling in at Camp Bouse. They were under the control of the 9th Tank Group Headquarters. The units appear in Table 1. Also attached to the 9th Tank Group was Company B, 220th Engineers of the 20th Armored Division.

Table 1. Units arriving at Camp Bouse by mid-September

Tank Battalion Medium (Special)	Commanding Officer	Authorized Strength	Departure to Camp Bouse	Arrival at Camp Bouse
736th	Lt. Col. William H. Dodge	669	4 Sept. from Ft Knox, KY	8 September
748th	Lt. Col. Robert R. Glass	669	15 July, from Ft Knox, KY	1 September
Other Units				
526th Armored Infantry Battalion	Lt. Col. Carlisle B. Irwin	998	From Ft. Knox, KY	13 Sept.
538th Ordnance Co. (HM Tk)		201		13 Sept.
150th Station Hospital (50 bed)	Maj. Camillo F. Mueller	41	Camp Wheeler, Georgia	31 August
Hq & Hq Co, 9th Tank Group	Lt. Col. Joseph H. Gilbreth	83	16 August	20 August

The phone conversation from Lt. Col. Rubel allows us to infer that camp was not ready for full operations by mid-September. Probably for that reason, half of the 736th Tank Battalion was furloughed for two weeks. The second half received their furloughs after the others returned. During this time, some of those remaining in camp were placed on Special Duty with the 9th Tank Group Headquarters to provide manpower to operate the utilities and security. In addition, since the 220th Engineers had to return to their parent unit, the units left in Camp Bouse finished up construction of the maintenance shop and school building. To do this they worked every evening and on weekends.

There was an inevitable delay in training, but by Monday, 11 October 1943, training began for the 748th and 736th Tank Battalions and the 526th Armored Infantry Battalion. In a letter to Brig. General Pierce, dated 18 October, Col. Gilbreth anticipated that a number of preliminary training tasks needed attention before moving to battle training. Numerous interruptions had prevented completion of small unit training. It would take several more weeks to correct the deficiencies the 9th Tank Group had found through its testing. In addition, new Tables of Organization would accompany the change to special battalions which meant more time needed for familiarization with new arms.

Col. Gilbreth also noted that the 740th Tank Battalion was lagging the other battalions in its training. He wrote "I will intensify their training in an effort to catch them up eventually with the other two (2) Tank Battalions, but hesitate to push them to the extent that they will fail to be thoroughly grounded in the fundamentals of a Tank Platoon (fighter or special) prior to the entry into company training and feel very strongly that it is only by having well trained platoons that larger units may expect success in battle." Col.Gilbreth set 15 November as the start time for special training, assuming special equipment would be delivered by then.

In fact, the first shipment of eight leaflets arrived October 24 and the next shipment arrived October 30. Captain Byran H. Rogers, S-3, arrived at Camp Bouse on Wednesday, November 3, on a long-term inspection trip from Fort Knox. He had instructions from Colonel Peploe to "observe everything to do with Special equipment and Special Training and to offer any assistance possible." By the night of November 4, the leaflets were tested for mechanical condition of the heaters [*i.e., the lights. Ed.*]. By the next night, twelve leaflets were ready for the field.

Captain Rogers reported that these were divided into platoons of 5, 4, and 3. "Heat control" *[operation of the light]*, he wrote, was very poor and the intervals much too great although sequence orders were performed very well. "This will easily be remedied by the use of the wobble plates now ready for operation." [Wobble plates, simulated tank movement. Carsie Denning Sr., personal communication.]

Captain Rogers reported that "the first phase of instruction was for maintenance personnel from the 736th Tank Battalion, the 748th Tank Battalion, and the 538th Ordnance Company. Tuesday, November 9, the second maintenance course starts for nineteen officers and men to be followed by one day of instruction for thirty-six officers and men in First and Second Echelon Maintenance of the Unit." He noted a list of deficiencies on the leaflets and forwarded a tentative schedule for Special Training for a period of six weeks to be followed by Group Maneuvers. This would apply to the 748th and 736th Tank Battalions.

In his last paragraph he states, "In conclusion there is a necessity for the S.T.G. (Special Training Group at Fort Knox) to stress the training of platoon leaders and company commanders in the handling of leaflets to facilitate the Group's 2nd Period of Training. It will be necessary because of the extensive use of the 108 leaflets to have at least one year's set of spare parts for one hundred tanks shipped out here before December 5."

DECLASSIFIED
Authority *140 88754*
By *PT* NARA Date *11/16/11*

~~SECRET~~

Demonstration
9th Tank Group
Camp Bouse, Arizona

DATE   : 11 November 1943

TIME   : 2300

WEATHER : Full moon - clear

PRESENT : Major General Gillem, Colonel Gilbreth, J. H., Colonel Miller,
J.J., Colonel Hall, F.F., Lt. Colonel Rubel, Major Hughes,
Captain Rousmaniere, James A., Captain Rogers, Byron H., 1st
Lieutenant Fetherston, John E., 9th Tank Group Headquarters.
748th Tank Battalion, 736th Tank Battalion, 740th Tank Battalion, 526th Armored Infantry Battalion, 538th Ordnance Company,
554th Ordnance Company, 150 Station Hospital Detachment.

EQUIPMENT: 11 - Leaflets and crews
            10 - M4 fighter tanks and crews
             1 - Peep - Platoon leaders
            19 - Half-tracks personnel carriers
             1 - Company Armored Infantry
             2 - M 16 Anti-aircraft carriers
             4 - 60" searchlights
             5 - 30 calibre machine guns
            20 - M1 rifles 30 calibre
             1 - 37mm sub calibre
            18 - M4 tanks as artillery and crews
           741 - 75mm ammunition, M 48 normals
           185 - 75mm ammunition super
          9600 - 30 calibre tracer ammunition
           980 - 50 calibre tracer ammunition
             1 - Jungle Jeep, Battalion Company vehicle
             1 - Half-track, Battalion Company vehicle (spare)
             3 - Leaflet spares
               - M 4 spares
               - Loud speaker system
               - Tank silouettes
               - L targets
            33 - Grenades, fragmentation
               - M 4 Projector, signal

OBJECTIVE: The demonstration was planned with two things in mind one to
acquaint the personnel of the 9th Tank Group with the special
weapon, its use and effect. Secondly, it was necessary to
start developing basic tactical doctrine.

- 1 -  ~~SECRET~~

~~SECRET~~

FORMATION: The demonstration was divided into two phases the first,
the spectators in the enemy position firing at the Leaflets.
The second phase, the spectators were approximately 400 yards
from the flank of the objective. Attached is a diagram of
the demonstration showing formation and coordination. The
formation used consisted of 11 leaflets in line at 40 yard
intervals with 10 M 4 gun tanks one between each leaflet.
One Company of Armored Infantry supported this attack mounted
in half-tracks. The headquarters rifle platoon acted as grenade throwers in the first wave followed by two succeeding waves
of infantry. Eighteen M4A1 tanks were used as supporting
artillery located 3080 yards from the 1st objective. Twenty
riflemen with M1 rifles, five .30 cal. machine guns, and one
37mm anti-tank gun were in position in front of the spectators,
with orders to commence firing as soon as the leaflets opened
the gates. Each rifleman had a clip of eight (8) rounds of
.30 calibre M1 tracer, each machine gun a belt of 50 rounds,
tracer and the 37mm anti-tank gun was equipped with sub-calibre
device. A total of 425 rounds were fired, concentrating on the
five leaflets on the left flank with the following results:

                Leaflet #1 - 5 hits - 1-4" from slot
                                      1-side of hull door
                                      1-on 75mm shield
                                      1-right-front fender
                                      1-support roller trunion

                Leaflet #2 - 7 hits - 1-4" from the slot
                                      1-6" from the slot
                                      2-8" from the slot
                                      2-4" from turret gun mount
                                      1-top of turret

                Leaflet #3 - 3 hits - 1-right front fender
                                      1-7" from slot
                                      1-top of left side of turret

                Leaflet #4 - 8 hits - 1-10" from slot
                                      1-12" from slot
                                      2-15" from slot
                                      1-top of turret
                                      1-drivers hatch
                                      1-grouser box
                                      1-left front fender

                Leaflet #5 - 4 hits - On front of turret none nearer
                                      to the slot than 9"

- 2 -

~~SECRET~~

The firing started when leaflets left light up line 800 yards from spectators but most of the hits were registered when leaflets approached the 150-200 yard mark, prior to this the majority of the gunners were shooting high. The riflemen and machine gunners were from the Armored Infantry Battalion none of whom had seen leaflet operation before. Formation moved at 5 miles per hour.

CONCLUSION: The slot is extremely hard to hit. It was impossible to lay on the source with any degree of accuracy even though the gunners were not under fire. Scatter proved harder to lay on than heat. Range estimation impossible to any degree of accuracy.

PHASE NO. 2

The form up line was 100 yards in the rear of the M 16, AA guns and searchlights. Heat came on as soon as the leaflets reached the AA line at which time the searchlights came on and the AA opened fire. The formation proceeded 200 yards on heat at which time the artillery which had been firing for 6 minutes lifted to 2nd objective 500 yards beyond. As soon as the artillery lifted, the leaflets and gun tanks started firing machine guns and 75mm using direct fire tracer ammunition. This was on scatter. When the formation came within 200 yards of the objective they halted, and the grenade throwers dismounted and proceeded to within 25 yards of the objective. By the time the last grenade had been thrown the second wave of infantry had advanced to the grenade throwers position. They were followed by the third wave, mopping up operations were continued by each wave, which proceeded to the screen line approximately 100 yards beyond objective. After the third wave had assaulted the positions the anti-tank platoon advanced with the 37mm anti-tank guns towed by half-tracks. Artillery ceased fire after 2 minutes on second objective.

CONCLUSIONS:

1. Artillery did not lift in time for dust to clear. Tank gunners were unable to see targets on objective.

2. Infantry advancing must stay in the cloak at all times.

3. Leaflets might have to advance with the last wave of infantry instead of remaining stationary.

4. Gun tanks and all supporting units must keep in line with leaflets. Platoon leader slightly to rear of formation, due to dust conditions of that terrain.

5. Very little other information was gained in this demonstration. It was evident that with the fire laid down by artillery and the direct fire of leaflets and gun tanks plus the dazzling effect of the beams, the enemy would have great difficulty in laying on advancing leaflets.

- 3 -

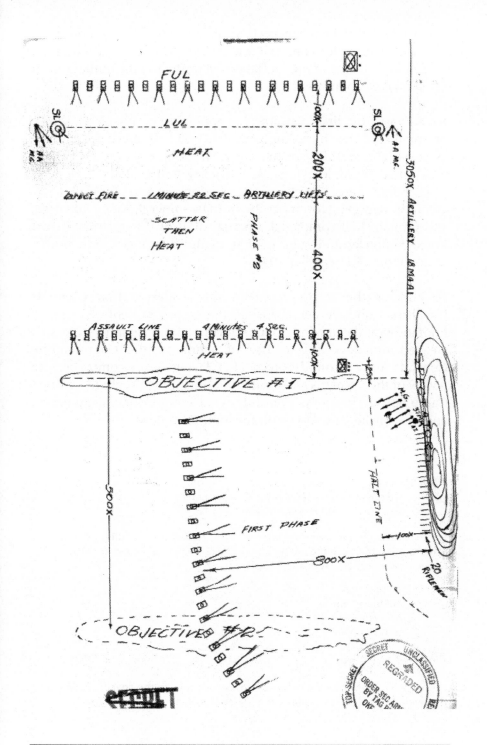

Major General Gillem's inspection of training at Camp Bouse left him with two major concerns: the lack of a doctrine detailing the actual employment of the special leaflet units, and the limitations of the special weapon itself.

To address the first concern, he appointed a board of senior Armored Officers, including ones who had observed the project overseas. The president of the board was Major Paul J. Ritchie. He was joined by Major Floyd W. Townsley and Captain C. F. Kell. Consultants were Colonel F. M. Thompson and Colonel J. H. Gilbreth. Between November 29 and December 9, Major Townsley and Captain Kell completed a partial draft of the doctrine at Fort Knox, Kentucky and submitted it to the board at Camp Bouse, Arizona, on 13 December 1943.

To address the second concern, he requested that Generals Eisenhower and Devers reconsider the project in light of its many limitations and changing circumstances. (See paragraph 3.c. below.) He recommended this course of action to the Commanding General, Army Ground Forces, after laying out a comprehensive review of the strengths and limitations, including his observations at Camp Bouse. The analysis portion of his report (four of eight pages) and his conclusions and recommendations follow:

20 November 1943

SUBJECT: "Cassock" Project
TO: Commanding General, Army Ground Forces,
         Army War College, Washington 25, D.C.

1. Pursuant to instructions contained in letter to the Commanding General, Armored Command, dated 21 September 1943, the undersigned submits herewith a report covering subject project.

       a. Historical
       b. Equipment
       c. Personnel
       d. Training

2. Analysis of Project

a. The undersigned to date has been uninstructed as to the specific nature of the overall operation into which the "Cassock" project will be injected.

Whatever the nature of the overall operation, the limitations of the project are so critical that the local circumstances under which it is employed must satisfy these limitations.The extreme secrecy with which the project has been screened, together with total absence of a similar means on the field of battle, indicates clearly that its use should involve a complete strategical surprise.

b. Tactical Powers:

The characteristic with the greatest potential value is that the project may offer the means of effecting tactical surprise. From present indications it appears to be the only means of providing moving illuminations for the continuance of a fire fight, which otherwise might be halted by darkness, or greatly decelerated. Thus the commander possessing this weapon can strike and capture a critical objective at a propitious moment, for instance at a moment when the enemy might logically expect a lessening of pressure, due to the termination of daylight.

The effect on morale of this unexpected weapon cannot be determined, but with the addition of unexpected weapons of another sort, such as a group of flame throwers mounted on tanks, it would seem reasonable that even the best trained troops would be alarmed.

The characteristic of surprise can also be effected by using this weapon to exploit a break-through. A commander with a new weapon has a definite advantage, for the enemy, faced with an unknown problem at his most desperate moment, may break. Complete rout under such circumstances might well result.

The training program for leaflet units obviously stresses operations under cover of darkness. By specialization a far better night performance could be expected from this type unit than from a normal tank element, due consideration being given to the fact that the tank is an M3 Medium with limitations inherent thereto in the position of the 75mm gun. Thus the completion of the routine training incident to this project prepares a unit for battle under night conditions. The combined phase of training is most important for it is only with the cooperation of air, other tanks, engineers, artillery, and infantry that an attack can be maintained.

c. Tactical Limitations:

The greatest limitation of the project is the sensitivity of the leaflets to natural conditions. The terrain selected as a scene of operations must be reasonably flat and treeless. Inequalities of ground will result in dispersal of illumination. Likewise the soil covering should not be too sandy or powdered. Dust obviously will be a deterrent even in a light wind. Care must be exercised in reference to time and place artillery concentrations are executed in order not to interfere with complete success of the illumination feature of the project. Observation of units training at Camp Bouse indicates that these close-in artillery concentrations and leading tanks in the cloak raise so much dust that leaflets lose their direction of attack and become confused. However, when the artillery concentrations are lifted, the position must be subjected to intense small arms fire in order to exploit the effect of the artillery fire.

Fog adversely affects all light. Therefore, any operation involving leaflets should be in an area free from sudden and intense fog. Rain, depending on the intensity, would lessen the effectiveness of the leaflet. Wind direction is vitally important because of its effect on dust.

Extreme care must be exercised in the protection of an exposed flank as vehicles in the darkened cloaks are clearly silhouetted to any observation from the flanks. Flanks may be protected by echeloning leaflets which are so sighted to blind such observation, or smoke could be used providing the wind direction is favorable.

Second to the limitations imposed by terrain and weather is the short range of the illumination. Tests at Fort Knox show the effectiveness to be up to 1200 yards only. This extremely short range requires an approach march, which must proceed almost within rifle fire of the enemy. Extreme care will have to be exercised in masking the approach to a suitable jump-off position, preferably by suitable terrain feature or the use of smoke under favorable atmospheric conditions, combined with noise to blank out characteristic sounds of the tanks.

It is again emphasized that the key to the success of this project is combined training with the air, infantry, artillery and engineers. The dark areas between vehicles are utilized to mask the presence of supporting troops.

The undersigned has attempted to gain information from such sources as are available as to the type of operations envisioned for this project. In most instances the rupture of a heavily fortified area has been indicated. The defenses of such an area present obstacles which it would seem inadvisable to attack with this weapon. Undoubtedly, defensive artillery fire will be heavy. Mine fields and tank traps would imperil progress. In any case the use of the weapon must be preceded by an air cover in order that the approach march will be reasonably safe. Air cover during the operation will be required.

All of the above seems to indicate that the best use of the leaflet will be in an open and unfortified area, or where there is a possibility of exploiting a break-through and creating panic in rear areas. This weapon should not be frittered away. It should be saved for the time and place where success will mean the attainment of a critical objective of major importance. This being a night attack, it must meet the utmost in simplicity of plan, careful preparation, secrecy, surprise, and cohesion in execution which are prerequisites to a successful night attack.

3. Conclusions:

        a. The undersigned understands that the initial employment of these units will be coordinated with like British units en masse to achieve strategical success, probably in Continental Europe. However, in view of the fact that both Generals Eisenhower and Devers recommended the adoption of this Special Project when functioning in assignments different from their current commands, it is my considered opinion that both should be advised as to when the units will be available.

        b. That, pending recommendations from the Commander of the European Theater of Operations, this project be pushed to the utmost with a view to the completion of training and shipment of all units overseas at the earliest practicable date.

        c. The tank elements involved in this project are receiving training which will permit their utilization in normal tank roles and with normal tank equipment after a relatively short period of modified training. Therefore, regardless of the continuance of the project, the training of units for the special project will provide tank units well versed in night training and operations.

        d. The decision to utilize "Cassock" units must be carefully evaluated and synchronized fully with weather, terrain, and enemy morale. Areas in which fogs are prevalent or rains heavy are not conducive to success with this weapon. Dusty or sandy terrain will, in general, jeopardize the attainment of surprise.

        e. This weapon should be injected into battle only when a strategical objective of great value is involved, for the duration of complete surprise cannot be predicted and counter measures will be promptly instituted.

        f. That not more than 108 leaflet tanks be shipped to Camp Bouse; that the remaining 392 leaflet tanks be assembled at a depot for shipment direct to the theater of employment at the earliest practicable date.

g. That the training of replacements mentioned in par. 1 c
(2) above, be conducted in the theater to which the Special
Training Group will be transferred.

4. Recommendations:

a. That the Commanding Generals of the European and North
African Theaters of Operations be advised as to when the units
will be available.

b. That units assigned to this project be shipped overseas at
earliest practicable date after training is completed.

c. That this project be continued pending advice from the
overseas theaters involved.

d. That the inherent limitations of employment of this project
be carefully considered before decision for its utilization
is reached.

e. That this weapon be injected into battle initially only when far
reaching strategical success is in the offing.

f. That leaflets for training at Camp Bouse be limited to 108.

g. That replacements be trained in the theater of employment.

A.C. GILLEM, JR.
Major General, U. S. Amy,
Commanding

For the benefit of the Commanding General, Major General Gillem
summarized where training stood at Camp Bouse. Two new units
had arrived since mid-October. The 740th Tank Battalion had finished its training at Fort Knox on 17 October and the 554th
Ordnance Company (HM) had cleared Fort Knox on 10 November
1943. The 701st Tank Battalion would be transferred to Camp Bouse
about 5 December once it finished its special training at Fort Knox.
The 738th Tank Battalion would follow about 27 December once
completing its special training at Knox. The 739th Tank Battalion,
located at Yakima, Washington, was being prepared to transfer to
Fort Knox about 10 December for special training.

The 10th Tank Group Headquarters and Headquarters Detachment was being transferred from Yakima, Washington to the California-Arizona Maneuver Area. It was to enter special training at Camp Bouse during December 1943 or early January 1944. General Gillem thought the 748th and 736th Tank Battalions, the 538th Ordnance Co (HM) (Tk), and the Hq & Hq Detachment, 9th Tank Group, would be ready for overseas movement by 1 March. They would be followed after 10 April by the 740th and 701st Tank Bns, the 526th Armd Inf Bn, and the 554th Ord Co (HM) (Tk).

Hq & Hq Det, 10th Tank Group, the 738th and 739th Tank Battalions would be ready by 24 May 1944. The 150th Station Hospital was to follow or accompany the last units ordered overseas. (Gillem Ltr to CG, AGF, Subject: "Cassock" Project, 20 Nov 1943. National Archives.)

Continuation of training

By 11 December, an eight week training schedule was in place. Each week included 44 hours of training for a total of 352 hours. According to this plan, the 736th and 748th Tank Battalions would begin their third week of training on 17 December. They would be making use of the CDL pamphlet. Objectives were organized for the Entire Company as well as more specific objectives for the Tank Sections and Maintenance Sections. Col. Gilbreth emphasized that unit training objectives include:

> • Familiarity with battle procedure areas including
> the Forward Assembly Area (FAA), Forming Up Position
> (FUP), Forming Up Line (FUL), Infantry Start Line (ISL),
> Lighting Up Line (LUL), and Assault Line (AL) *[Note that
> Captain Rogers uses some of these abbreviations in his sketch
> of the 11 November demonstration for General Gillem. Ed.]*

• Instruction on tactical procedures to include:

(1) attack of a hasty fortified position,

(2) crossing a defile or bridge,

(3) continuance of a battle which would normally be broken off at dusk,

(4) attack against armor,

(5) attack of a mobile force in a harassing or pursuit role,

(6) defense against night attacks on a fortified position,

(7) counter attack over known ground.

As an example of the platoon level drill, we found a document in the archives that describes the functions of the crew in detail:

<u>General:</u>

Initials: _____ 3d-1
Date: 30 NOV 43

During this training various drill movements that may have a tactical application are taught and should also blend together the platoon under the leadership of the commander who will be leading them in action. Although it is realized that some of the drill movements taught may seldom be used in action, the training derived from them is such that it will make the platoon flexible, and if unusual circumstances arise in action they will be capable of carrying out any unusual formation or maneuver on the orders of the Platoon Commander without previous practice in that formation or maneuver.

The principles taught in class and lecture rooms and during individual field training should be continually stressed in Platoon Drill and should be and automatic application when this training has been completed.

<u>Object:</u>

(1) To practice the three principles of Leaflet operation:
    (a) Illumination of the objective.
    (b) Concealment of assaulting troops.
    (c) Hampering the enemy in the use of his weapons.

(2) To teach platoon and other commanders, drivers and operators the orders required to carry out the various drill movements.

(3) To practice crews as a team and the platoon as a team.

<u>Crew:</u>

There are five members in a Leaflet crew and are:- Leaflet Commander, Driver, Operator, Gunner, Assistant Gunner. The ideal is that each should be interchangeable, but at least the gunner should be capable of Leaflet driving and the assistant gunner of Leaflet operating. - The Leaflet Commander should know how to drive and operate.

The duties of the crew are:-

(1) Leaflet Commander:
    (a) Gives orders to his crew so that the correct position of his vehicle is maintained in the formation.
    (b) Correct the position of the heat if necessary.
    (c) Indicate targets to and control the fire of the gunner.
    (d) Responsible for all radio communications.
    (e) That all orders of his platoon commander are carried out.

(2) Driver:-

    (a) Responsible for keeping direction to maintain the light intensity on the objective.
    (b) Maintenance of a correct interval and station so that the width of the objective is completely illuminated, that cloaks are provided for the attacking troops and to prevent penetration of the light screen.
    (c) A constant speed during the advance and the overcoming of obstacles that would be avoided in normal tank driving.

(3) Operator:-

    (a) Maintenance of the heat on the objective by correct manipulation of the elevating and depressing gear in anticipating the ground and by traversing.
    (b) Clean and quick changes of timing sequence on the orders of the platoon commander.
    (c) The maintenance of the cloak in cooperation with the driver.
    (d) Keep the hester in action.

(4) Gunner:-

    (a) Receives practice in locating targets as illuminated by the heat and aiming his gun at them.

SECRET

(5) Assistant Gunner:-

(a) Receives practice in maintaining the gun in action.

(6) The Platoon Commander is responsible for:-

(a) The direction and speed of the platoon.
(b) The giving of orders for the execution of all maneuvers.
(c) Location and recognition of objectives.
(d) The opening and cessation of fire.
(e) The formation adopted and that it is maintained.

Composition of a Platoon:

A platoon consists of:-

(a) One command vehicle for the Platoon Commander.
(b) Four active Leaflets. These are numbered or lettered from right to left and No. 2 or "B" Leaflet is known as the guide Leaflet and in the event of the Platoon Commander becoming a casualty, guide will take control and be responsible for the speed, direction, changes of timing sequence according to previous instructions and also for general control of the platoon. Guide will also be responsible for speed and direction if the Platoon Commander decides to change his position in the formation.

In the event of the six Leaflets being used during an attack, No. 3 is then the guide Leaflet. This is because the right center is the best position for other Leaflets to follow for direction and speed. If the guide becomes a casualty, his duties are taken over by the left center Leaflet.

(c) Two mechanical reserve Leaflets who travel approximately 30 yards behind the formation and are Nos. 5 and 6. They will act on the orders of the Platoon Commander in replacing casualties or in the boosting of the illumination, or for flank protection. They must be capable of taking the place of any of the active Leaflets.

PROCEDURE:

The procedure to start and stop a formation, make changes of timing sequence is usually given over the R/T but training in watching for changes of sequence as given by the guide Leaflet should be practiced to overcome the eventuality of a radio breakdown.

(The executive word "NOW" is the equivalent to "OUT" in normal R/T working)

(a) To start a formation on the move:- "Hullo Crossbar, this is Crossbar X Ray, Prepare to advance--Advance--Now."
(b) "Hullo Crossbar, this is Crossbar X Ray. Prepare to open gates--Open gates--Now".
(c) Hullo Crossbar, this is Crossbar X Ray. Prepare for Scatter --Scatter--Now".
(d) "Hullo Crossbar, this is Crossbar X Ray. Prepare for heat-- Heat--Now".
(e) To extinquish:- "Hullo Crossbar, this is Crossbar X Ray, Prepare for Close gates--Close gates--Now".

In giving orders with the use of the word "Now" as executive, a slight pause should be made before the executive word.

From all accounts, training proceeded satisfactorily. More passes were granted around Christmas, giving the men an opportunity for a recreational convoy expedition to Hollywood and Los Angeles. The photo below was taken at the Paladium, across from the Biltmore Hotel.

LEFT TO RIGHT: Joe Denmarsh, Art Alexander, Dave Fitzpatrick, Jim Kane

By early January, at the highest levels of command, attention began shifting to preparations for the movement out of Camp Bouse to overseas. Col. James C. Fry, G-3 Section, Headquarters Armored Command, Fort Knox, Kentucky was ordered to Camp Bouse to act "as a representative of the Commanding General, Armored Command." In the document below, one of the expectations placed on Col. Fry was to bring all the units up to T/O (Table of Organization) strength with the approved over-strength to take casualties into account. He was also responsible for tests to determine the readiness of all units for completing their training. If problems were to occur, he was to "settle as many questions as possible on the ground in accordance with existing regulations and common sense."

SECRET

HEADQUARTERS ARMORED COMMAND
Office of the Commanding General
Fort Knox, Kentucky

320.2 (S) GNOCS   31 December 1943.

SUBJECT: Special Training Project.

TO   : Colonel James C. Fry, G-3 Section, Headquarters Armored Command.

1. Orders are being issued directing that you, with assistants, proceed to Camp Bouse, Arizona. During your stay, you will act as a representative of the Commanding General, Armored Command. It is desired that you see that the following is accomplished:

    a. Adjustment be made of available personnel within and between all units under the jurisdiction of this headquarters so that all organizations are filled to T/O strength with proportionate over-strength in both officers and men. For this, you will make use of all personnel except men who are obviously unsuited for any service. In this connection, see Circular 293, War Department, and the attached copy of letter General Pierce to Colonel Riley Ennis, dated 24 December.

    b. See that the responsible commanders prepare units for over-seas movement on dates to be furnished by this headquarters.

    c. Require such training tests to be made to determine the status of training of all units with a view to determining whether or not training is progressing satisfactorily, and to the end that they will complete training requirements prior to readiness for overseas movement.

    d. When a unit is alerted, require that the company commander prepares the status report required by Army Ground Forces and that it is certified by the battalion and group commander concerned.

    e. See that necessary equipment adjustments are made so that the maximum benefit can be obtained, and see that all personnel concerned understand how to do this.

    f. Settle as many questions as possible on the ground in accordance with existing regulations and common sense.

2. It is desired that you operate through command channels, however, you are authorized to issue such orders as are necessary in the name of the Commanding General, Armored Command.

                 By command of Major General SCOTT:

                                 JOHN L. PIERCE,
                                 Brigadier General,
                                 Chief of Staff.

1 Incl:
    Ltr Gen Pierce to
    Col Ennis, 12-24-43.

SECRET

In January 1944, the total strength of the units at Camp Bouse was 5,265 personnel. Of these, 291 (5%) were officers. The units consisted of the 150th Station Hospital, 554th Ordnance Company, 538th Ordnance Company, 526th Armored Infantry Battalion, the Headquarters and Headquarters Company of the 9th Armored Group, and five Tank Battalions (Special). These were the 701st, 748th, 736th, 740th, and 738th. Shortly after, the 739th Tank Battalion (Special) was attached, adding another seven hundred or so troops.

By month's end Camp Bouse was hosting its full complement of troops. These consisted of both the 9th and 10th Armored Group Headquarters and Headquarters Companies, six Tank Battalions, one Armored Infantry Battalion (less one company already enroute overseas), two Ordnance Maintenance Companies, one Station Hospital which was being expanded from 50 to 150 beds, one detachment of Counter-Intelligence Corps people and the personnel from the Special Training Group from Fort Knox. The troops were divided into two Groups, each with its own headquarters.

The peak load was short-lived. On 30 January, the following units were put on alert for movement 1 March, with advanced detachments leaving early in February:

> Hq & Hq Co, 9th Armd Group (Col. Gilbreth)
> 748th Tank Bn, (Lt. Col. Glass)
> 736th Tank Bn, (Lt. Col. Dodge)
> 538th Ord Main Co (Capt Burke)

Seven units were relieved from attachment to the 9th Armored Group and attached to Headquarters 10th Armored Group, effective 30 January 1944. These units were:

> 526th Armored Infantry Battalion
> 150th Station Hospital
> 554th Ordnance (HM) (Tk)
> 701st Tank Battalion (M) (Sp)
> 738th Tank Battalion (M) (Sp)
> 739th Tank Battalion (M) (Sp)
> 740th Tank Battalion (M) (Sp)

On 3 February, the Provisional Overhead Company, Ninth Armored Group, which was constituted 24 November 1943, was dissolved. Colonel Fred Thompson, CO, 10th Armored Group, had left Camp Bouse for overseas. Lt. Col. Irwin, 526th AIB, became acting commander of the 10th Armored Group, consisting of all elements not alerted for 1 March. The 10th Armd Gp and Hq Co were to take over all camp functions being performed by the 9th Armd Gp Hq and Hq Co.

With training at Fort Knox completed, members of the Special Training Group were sent out to Camp Bouse to help with the transition. Those not ordered to join Col. Thompson would be transferred to units at Camp Bouse to travel overseas with those units. Carsie Denning was one of those attached to the 736th Tank Bn for overseas movement.

For a week in March, Lieut. Colonel William H. Dodge assumed command of the Ninth Armored Group. He was only a temporary appointment, and on 16 March 1944 Colonel J. H. Gilbreth took charge again.

CHAPTER 8

Oral Histories of Camp Bouse

Introduction

In this section, the editors share from the oral histories we have collected over the past two years. Most of the interviews took place by phone. We asked a set of questions worked out in advance of the interview. Each interview lasted approximately an hour. In every case we asked permission to record the interview. Then we transcribed the recording and mailed a copy to each person for comments, corrections, and ultimately their acceptance. Sometimes this involved sending a manuscript twice and later going over portions again by phone. In each case we secured a release for publication.

One decision was to keep the transcript as close as we could to the way the person spoke. This surprised some of the guys when they saw their language verbatim. We did this because the nature of oral history is that it is a spoken history, not carefully edited for an academic audience.

Their narratives help capture the spirit and atmosphere of life while training in the desert sixty years ago. The stories come together like a loose weaving. The documents from the last chapter establish event chronology. To keep the weaving metaphor, they are the warp threads. The oral histories in this chapter are the weft threads woven to complete the picture.

We begin this chapter with John J. Coveney's account, recorded in September 2003 at the reunion of the 736th Tank Battalion in Seattle, Washington. We were in the hospitality room and there was a lot of background noise, but his story comes through. It is particularly important since he is the only officer we have interviewed to date.

John J. Coveney, Headquarters Company, Platoon Leader, Reconnaissance Platoon. Interviewed 13 September 2003.

I was the recon officer in Headquarters Company of the 736 Tank Battalion during WWII. We formed at Camp Rucker, Alabama. I was the transportation officer and took them to Fort Knox, KY for special training. Then I brought them out to the desert to the railhead at Bouse. We detrained from there and struck out into the desert to Butler Valley.

What did I know about deserts? I'm from Massachusetts.

It was so damn hot you could fry an egg on the palm of your hand. But anyway, I was a second lieutenant and when you're a second lieutenant you're the lowest of the low. An occasion arose after we had organized and tentage put up and so forth. We were going to have a maneuver. I got to tell you this story because it followed me.

We had an operations officer that was in the brigade. He laid out this whole live fire project. His name was Paul J. Ritchie. He was a major at that time. Before you have a live fire exercise you make sure that there are a lot of safety precautions. You know where everybody is, what they are supposed to do, and so forth. And he gave this briefing and I, being a recon officer, and being very familiar with the use of maps, when he got through he asked if there were any questions.

I stuck my paw up in the air. He said, "What is it?"

I said, "Has anybody checked the coordinates?"

He said, "What coordinates?"

I said, "Well, the impact area and where my troop is located are both the same!"

He said, "Well, we'll take care of that."

He walked by me about ten minutes later and he says, "Lieutenant, you're never going to live long enough to regret what you just did."

So OK, I let it go off my shoulder and I forgot about it. But I didn't know what rank could do to a second lieutenant. Well, in any event, the exercise went off, things were straightened out, nobody got hurt.

Six months later we were in Wales. And who is the new battalion commander but Paul J. Ritchie! So my sergeant, who had been in the regular army, says, "Lieutenant, time for you to put in for a transfer."

I said, "OK, that makes sense to me."

He [Paul J. Ritchie] refused to allow me to transfer and said I was one of the best officers that he had. Looks great on the report, but what was behind it was "I'm going to get that son-of-a-bitch."

I never got promoted until I had been overseas six months and Congress said anybody that was overseas was automatically pro-moted. And he congratulated me and I said, "No thanks to you, sir. The Congress of the United States gave me a promotion."

I got my silver bar, but you know, the war went on and we were attached to the 78th Infantry Division in the Huertgen Forest. That was murder. We were sitting still, holding a defensive position, and the Germans knew every inch of the ground and they were shooting at us. We didn't know what was on the other side of the hill! And we were trying to defend ouselves…but you said you wanted to hear about Camp Bouse.

I'll tell you about when I was sent out to do some road work. The road that went from the railhead into where the camp was, was a very, very good road because the engineers had got there before I got there. They were sent there to sink a well, which they did. I mean, it gushed water beyond their ability to control it. It was almost like an artesian well. You should have seen the grass grow. They finally got a cap put on and they put lines down to the company streets so the mess halls could be on a company street, and north of that they had tentage for the enlisted men and the officers.

We had to build ranges. So, because I was supposed to know about roads and bridges and so forth because I was a recon officer, I got appointed. Now, fortunately, we had a bulldozer and a bucket-type earth mover, so the first range I built was a machine gun range for firing live ammunition from a tank to tow targets that were in the revetment I had dug for the targets. This was in the camp area, about 8 or 900 yards from the westerly side of the camp going toward the Colorado River.

I built that, so they wanted me to build a moving machine gun range for the half-tracks. This Colonel Rubel showed up. Citizen of Arizona. He said to lay the lanes out so none of the Saguaro cactus would get destroyed. I did so. I had to move the lanes at different distances apart so I could adhere to what he requested. Next time we put on a firing problem—where the hell do you think the men shot? They shot at the Saguaro cactus! Which was inevitable!

Then I had to lay out roads across the desert so that the tanks could go out and have a pattern of roads they could maneuver on. So I had a sergeant, Minks. Floyd Minks. He came from North Dakota and he worked for the county road department. So I told him we had to build these roads, and he said, we'll need a transit and we'll need this and that and so on. I asked for that and they told me it wasn't in the TO&E *[Table of Organization and Equipment. Ed.]* so therefore you don't get one.

So I said to Sergeant Minks, "What are we going to do?"

He says, "Let's get a tripod and put a board on the top of it and we'll use the straight edge as an alidade." He flagged the lanes. We got the road grader out and made a crown for the road and went from one side of the valley to the other side of the valley. Now we had roads. Then they decided we needed a new road to Wendon. So I got elected to build a new road. We had to go through some rock. You couldn't push it aside. So they gave me a requisition for some TNT so I could blast. Fortunately I had had some exposure to explosives because my father was a cartographer for the Commonwealth of Massachusetts, building the Corbin Reservoir. He told me all about the difference between black powder and dynamite, what the characteristics were, so we blasted our way through Cunningham Pass.

There were some mines out there. We got rid of the miners because the department of Army didn't want anybody around there because of these tanks that had the lights on them. We were told not to talk about it. It wasn't until I got to Europe when they decided they could-n't use the tanks therefore they re-issued us M4 tanks with 75mm guns on them and put the CDL tanks off in a field—now you could talk about it. But nobody would believe me anyway. The after action report never mentions CDL, only "Medium Special" tanks. The only mention is when we were in Wales and were going to France, there is a notation that we had to turn in all the special tanks. We had a reunion in Louisville and went out to Fort Knox, Kentucky. There was a sergeant on the stage going on about the history of Fort Knox and so forth, and he asked "Does anybody have any questions?"

One of the sergeants stands up and says, "How about the Gizmo?"

"The what?"

"The Gizmo!"

"Never heard of it."

Now at Knox, they have a Gizmo. It's marked "the Gizmo" but there is nothing that says what we did with it, how we used it, etc.

Let me tell you about my military career. I had a choice. I joined the Army before Pearl Harbor. That was the regular Army. I rose to the rank of a buck sergeant. But I knew a general officer because I evac-uated his wife, sister-in-law, and his daughter from Hickham Field on December 7, not knowing who they were. Somebody told me, "Get a car and evacuate all the women and children!" So I hotwired a car, because I didn't have keys to any car, and this woman asked me what my name was. I was a corporal at that time and one day I get a messenger from General Higgenberger that he'd like to speak to me. So I reported to the general and he thanked me for what I had done for his wife! When the conversation was all over, he said "Young man, if there is anything I can do for you, you don't have to go through channels, you can come and knock on my door." He was from South Boston. And I'm from Dorchester, which years ago was South Boston. His son was appointed to West Point by John McCormack, Speaker of the House. And he asked me if I knew John McCormack and I said he's a friend of the family. He said, "We're both in the same boat." He offered to send me to school in Miami, Florida,

because they were starting an administrative school for the Air Force, because the Air Force was being formed at that time, from Army Air Corps. I says, "Flying a desk, this isn't going to cut much mustard in my neighborhood when the war's over. I'm not interested."
"Well," he says, "I'll talk to you later."

Then one day he called me and he said "Some dumb damn fool general thinks they're going to win the war with tanks. Would you go to Fort Knox?"

I said, "I'll go any place."

He says, "I think his name is Patton."

I've been the most fortunate person ever because when I got out of the service I knew that if I stayed in, keeping my commission, I would have been subject to recall for ten years in the Army Reserve system. So I joined the Reserves. I'm a first lieutenant by this time and I joined an active unit in Pasadena, California, and the commanding officer, Major _____, asked me, "Do you think you could run a company?"

I said, "That's no problem."

"What do you mean, that's no problem?"

"When I was an enlisted man, I was a personnel clerk, I done this and I done that."

"OK," he says, "Headquarters Company. You're company commander." Lo and behold two months later, I'm a captain. Then I got to be a staff officer, and then I got command of my own battalion. The last five years before I retired, they were number one in the sixth army. They were, not me. They did the work. I gave them the incentive to get the reward. Loved it.

When I retired I was Chief of Staff of the 63rd Infantry Division. I was entitled to be promoted to a Bird Colonel, and then they deactivated the unit.

O.V. Coffman, "A" Company. Interviewed 13 October 2003.

When we got into Ozark I thought that was bad, but Gawd, when we pulled into this place called Bouse, Arizona, Lord have mercy! There wasn't nothin' there but a little depot, one grocery, and an old saloon across the street. We unloaded there and I believe the drivers and tank commanders stayed and drove the tanks in. The rest of us they loaded on trucks and took us in to this God-forsaken place that they called Butler Valley. We went over this big mountain and we fell down into this Butler Valley. God Almighty. There wasn't nothin' there. There wasn't nothin'! The engineers had come in and had started grading. They had roads cut out with a grader and they had areas graded out for each company, for you to put your tents up. They had tents all dumped all along for you to pitch. Next morning we started pitching tents, these big pyramidal tents—five men per tent—and first day we was pitchin' them, I got stung by a scorpion. He hit me on the side. I took my coveralls off and hung 'em up on the tent pole and the sergeant come by and made me put my coveralls on and when I pulled 'em up I felt something warm hit me on the side. I thought it was a buckle, a button on the outfit. Then a scorpion ran out the leg and one of the guys killed it. They took me over and lanced it and sucked out the poison, but then they give us furloughs.

Can you imagine? We'd been there about three days; they gave half the camp furloughs. Well, I'm all sore on the side but they give me a furlough; no money, you had to have your ticket before they'd issue your furlough. They took us into Phoenix—150 miles by them six by sixes—then you'd buy a ticket for a quarter, just so you had some kind of a ticket, then you had to wire home to get your money back. We got our tickets. I got home with a nickel in my pocket. Stayed home for nine days, had a good time, enjoyed myself. Got to eat some good food again, 'cause throughout basic training we ate fairly well but we started eating B's, C's, and K rations from the word "go." We ate a few "A" rations in basic training.

After we went back to the desert, I got into Phoenix and I was late getting back so I figured, "Well, I'm in a barrel of trouble here." But Phoenix as a hub, trains started coming in from all directions and they had to send a convoy in, there were so many of us guys AWOL.

So ol' me, always into something and doin' something, I went to the Red Cross and they told us this convoy was comin' in after us, so I go back downtown and lo and behold, I got drunk. Missed the convoy.

There I was in Phoenix, 150 miles from camp, AWOL, no way to get there so I asked the lady, "Is there any way you know for me getting back out there?"

She said, "I think there's a truck coming in here for some office equipment. He might let you ride with him."

He did. He let me ride with him, but I had to ride on the back of the truck, he wouldn't let me ride up front. I'd like to froze to death, 'cause, man, it got cold out there at night. So I rode back to camp and I'll never forget the next morning. We fell out for reveille and when that convoy got in I wasn't on it and they'd reported me absent without leave again. So when my platoon sergeant reported us "All present and accounted for," the First Sergeant jumped on that, "Alright buddy, Private Coffman ain't here by God, what are you going reporting everybody present?"

I said, "Well I'm here!"

He said, "How in the world did you do that?" He just couldn't understand it. I was always into something. I was a good soldier. I knew my job, but I was happy-go-lucky, just like I am now. I carried on, everybody knew me, and as a matter of fact, I guess I was pretty good. I was in the command tank. I was in Lt. Myers's tank. I was his gunner and we were number one tank. "A" Company was number one anyway. We pretty well spearheaded. We had an extra five inches of armor on our tanks because we did spearhead.

After we got coming back in off of furloughs—half the company went one time for fifteen days, then they come back, then the other half of the outfit went for fifteen days. So they got us all back and by that time we had the tents all up and the engineers had erected big barracks for the company commands and we had sidewalks. They were just gravel and they laid rocks like you've seen around army camps—I guess they're still out there. We made a nice city out there.

Those engineers, they did a heck of a job. It was a hell of a place, but it was quite a place when we got it going out there. They finally got water run. We could get water into our Lister bags in each area, got our tents, and finally some of us got stoves in the tents where we could get heat. They issued so much coal for each tent. We'd have trouble keeping up with the cold. Damn guys would steal your coal when you were out on a detail.

They had a laundry company, which was the 629 quartermaster and laundry company and they were stationed there in Bouse. So we'd just send our laundry out and it cost you so much a month.

After we got things pretty well situated then they come in with the Gizmos. We worked at night out there. It was so damn hot during the day we couldn't have worked with those lights in daytime anyway. We had a hell of a time trying to sleep. We worked all night with those lights. We had some places where we worked at Chocolate Drop Mountain. It's a wonder it's still there. We worked on that dude. I was a gunner and also I was an operator. I went to that operating school. I think they sent most of us gunners to that. With those M3 tanks you also had a 75mm gun on it. I believe we operated the lights and we used the 75 when we had to also. We had a .30 caliber up there with that light.

An armored searchlight is what it was. It had a 13 million beam candle power at the arc light. That's where the two arcs came together. That light was directed by a bunch of mirrors through a small slit in the turret. And it had a device on it we called a "shutter," which operated at a speed which caused the enemy's eyes to dilate and contract at a rate calculated to cause night blindness. Flicker and vertigo were also names they had with this thing. There was also a red and blue filter which helped impair one's judgment of distance. The red made the object appear near and the blue made the object appear farther away than it actually was. It got awful hot up there in a little bitty ol' place where you operated that thing.

The object was to attack enemy positions at night. In your attack formation you have your tanks about fifty foot apart. You shine them lights out there about 150 or 200 foot, these lights would cross and it would form a "cloak of darkness" and out in that cloak of darkness there would be a fighter tank. They couldn't see this tank, but it was there. The tank could see them but they couldn't see it.

We would work all night and then come in and have our meal. It wasn't breakfast, it was supper, just like you was comin' in from work. We were on strictly canned meats, cheese, "B" rations, everything was dehydrated. Vegetables were all dehydrated, powdered milk. No "A" rations, the good stuff like you get now. Everything was dehydrated in cans, and in our tanks we had a five-in-one ration, which was for five men, which we didn't use too much. You could get canned stuff out of it but they had a little Coleman burner for you to heat bacon. Hell, you never had a chance to get out and fry bacon. But anyway, it was there.

We trained with that Gizmo. We went into Phoenix if you were lucky enough to get a pass—we were pretty good on passes—you'd ride them convoys 150 miles in and spend one night, then ride 150 miles back. It was just good to get out. We had a lot of fun in Phoenix. It was a good town, but a very small town. I don't think it was about 30 or 40 thousand when we were down there. We were there for a reunion a few years back at Scottsdale—my God, that town is enormous. It's unbelievable.

One time, around Christmas, they wanted a volunteer from each company to go in as MP's. You'd get to stay in three nights for Christmas as the MP, and then you'd get to stay three nights at New Year's Eve on a pass. Well, old lucky me, I'm going to volunteer for that to go to Phoenix. I volunteered to go in on the first wave. I was going to be MP during the Christmas days for my outfit, then I was going to stay in for New Year's Eve.

Well, we got into town and they put you with two regular MP's. I'm the only guy in the outfit that got locked up. I got drunk and they locked me up. So Captain McCarthy, that was my company commander, he had to come down and get me the next morning at jail, and he told me, "Coffman, I swear, I don't know about you. What happened?"

I said, "Well, no sad story, I just got drunk."

He said, "Well, I tell you what I'm going to do. I oughta take you back to camp—ain't nothin' I could do to make it any worse than just send you back to camp, but I'm just going to let you stay in for the whole six days."

So I stayed six days. What a ball!

I was always into something like that. My tank crew—there was two of us guys—myself and Carlisle, he was my tank commander later on after Lt. Myers got killed in Kesternick. Carlisle and I were just like brothers. You see one of us, you saw the other one. We were together all the time. We were about the same size and everything. But we were always into something.

I'll tell you another little story about out there in the desert. One morning we came in from work and the meat we got was in cans. You got cheese in five-pound cans. You wasn't supposed to get those, those were supposed to be served at the mess hall. But I think every tent out there had one buried; something to eat on. You'd starve to death.

We come in one morning, it was just breaking day, so we went by for breakfast, which was supper. You had your dehydrated carrots, your cabbage and your potatoes and everything. This one particular time, the officers were settin' back behind the cooks at a table set up for them. You come by the tent and they had wood around it up to about three feet. And just like a drive-in restaurant, where you'd walk by and they would serve you above the wood. They raised the tent flap up and served us there.

So I had my mess kit up there, and this guy's name was "Red" Bradley, I'll never forget him. He put my vegetables in, we had Vienna sausage, cooked in tomato ketchup, so instead of putting my fruit cocktail on my lid up at the top on my mess kit, he just dumped it on top of my vegetables. I took that and I hit him right in the face with it. Damn, I hit him right in the face. And he hollered and turned around and the officers, with all that tomato ketchup runnin' down his face, they thought I'd cut his head off. They wanted to know what happened. He told them "Coffman threw his damn mess kit in my face." So it was one of those deals where

Lt. Myers came out and wanted to know what happened.

I told him. I said, "These cooks, you think they'd bought this damn food. They don't want to give you nothin' to eat ..." Boy he chewed him up one side and down the other one. I didn't get no details on that.

This old mule, 8-Ball, we used to take him over to the PX and get him drunk on 3.2 beer. Take a container and put the beer out and that mule would drink it and be walking back and I'd seen him just staggering. His legs would get tied up with each other, criss-crossed. He'd get loaded. He was company. That mule was company. You'd be walking guard and he'd come around with you.

One other time, we had a stockade. We had our own stockade for guys that went AWOL. We had two guys in it from "A" Company. They were worse than me. I never did get in the stockade—I lucked out. But anyway, one day on my detail I was to take them out on a work detail. So I had two of them. So I took them out on a work detail which was policing up the area, just keep 'em moving more or less. About two o'clock in the afternoon, boy, it was hot. I told them, "Now I'm going to take you back to the tent with me to get in out of the sun if you promise me you won't mess up or anything."

They said, "Yeah, let's get in the shade."

So we went back to the tent and I said, "While I'm here I'm going to take my gun down and clean it and then I won't have to do that tonight."

They set there and watched me take my gun down and get it all stripped, and they said, "We're going to the PX."

Damn, here they went. They took off to the PX and by the time I got over there I don't know how many beers they'd drank. It's a wonder they didn't put me in jail with them.

You had to have things like that to happen. If you didn't you'd have went wild. Roger, you can't imagine what a grind this was on us young guys 'till we got used to it—I don't think we ever really got used to it, but you just think, going to town, five men together. Here's a good one.

One of the boys in our outfit, his name was Norman Woods; he died about two months ago. Norman got shot up bad over there, it's a wonder he ever made it. A German on the second floor shot him right down through the top of the head. He went through all kinds of stuff. He was a big man; I don't see how he ever got in a tank. But anyway, while we were in Phoenix, he got married. His wife, Virginia, I'll never forget her, we spent the honeymoon with Virginia and Woods on a five-man buddy pass, all of us guys with 'em, in the room with 'em. She used to talk about that when we had these reunions. She said, "Coffman, I will never forget our honeymoon. Our wedding night, in the hotel room with you four other guys. What a ball." We were all drunk, we didn't let them sleep, we just kept them a-goin', was was up all night with 'em. It was something else.

I'll tell you another dumb thing I did once, coming back from Phoenix. We were about half drunk when we got on the trucks. Carlisle—they put him on one truck, and I was on the truck right behind him. Well, Carlisle had a pint of whiskey. We're going down the highway and I got—see, these 6 by 6's, the cabs were like a convertible, just had a canvas over them. So I got up to the cab with the truck driver and I asked him, I said, "Can you pull up and get your truck up real close to the back end of that other truck?"

He said, "What you going to do?"

I said, "Can you get up there and hold it? I want to get over in that truck."

Well, we're going down the highway about fifty miles an hour and he pulled that truck up to the back end of the other truck and I went out over the hood and climbed up and got up into the other truck to where Carlisle was with that bottle. Can you imagine tricks like that?

We left the desert and went to Camp Shanks and got on the Queen and went overseas and we went into a place that was just about as bad as Bouse, Arizona was. It was over in Wales, South Wales—we called it "sheep dip hill." Whew! Rain, snow, it was awful. We laid around there, worked with the tanks, and then with the invasion, went into France.

Vernon Tweit, "C" Company. Interviewed 10 October 2003.

The camp was being built by the soldiers who were at the camp. You'd get details for truck drivers. You wouldn't have any trouble getting volunteers to drive trucks, but then they'd say, "OK, your truck is that wheelbarrow over there. Pick it up." We'd be digging ditches and hauling dirt from one place to the other. We'd pick up rocks in the desert and bring them in to mark out areas. Mostly walks. They'd take you out in a truck and you'd bring them in by truck—wouldn't have to use a wheelbarrow.

I was a gunner. In the Gizmo it was very crowded! We had a crew of five. You've got your loader, who loads the "75." The "75" in the Gizmo only has a traverse of about 15 degrees left and right and you can get below level a few degrees and above level maybe 25 degrees. You had to move the tank to aim the gun. The gunner is sitting in a position along side of the gun. Your loader (assistant gunner) was behind you so he could load the gun, and your tank commander was in the turret. Then your driver was down in front. The operator was in the turret with the light, and was protected up there. They had to protect him. Thirteen million candlepower—that's like a welding arc.

The operator's job was really to control the shutters and everything up there, do the flashing, light the light and all that. The tank commander was a sergeant. The next in line was a corporal. That was the gunner. The driver—we called them "T-5's"—a technician corporal. (A T-5 is a corporal with a T under two chevrons). That was lower than a corporal. The assistant driver was a PFC or a private. That could have been your assistant gunner. The operator was a private.

The first time I saw that light we were out in Butler Valley. We were marched out to a small hill and when it got dark they told us the show was about to start. It was dark, black as pitch. We didn't know what we were getting in to. We heard this roar out in the far distance and we could hear the tanks moving but we couldn't see them. All of a sudden, the lights came on and they formed that "V" behind the lights where you had the infantry advancing in the darkness, then they started firing live ammunition. Not at us, but towards us. Scared the hell out of most of us! Then it was explained to us what the situation was, how things would work and what was expected of everybody.

That light was very dazzling. You try to look into it and you don't see anything. Most of our fieldwork after that was all at night. You'd do the maintenance and stuff that was needed during the daytime. Firing was done during the day, out on the firing range, but the light was strictly night work.

It was a short time later that we got our tanks and we were assigned as crews. We had to start cleaning guns and equipment and perform maintenance on them. They were M3 Grants. They had the 75mm mounted on the side over the right sponson. I was gunner the whole time. The gun was my responsibility. I remember one time we were cleaning the gun, pounding waste—cotton waste, any old rags, soaked up in soap and water—through the barrel of the gun with a long rammer staff to try to clean it. The rammer staff was about eight to ten feet long and had a brass fitting on the end. The waste got very tight and we were having trouble getting it through. So, I told the guys, "I'll go inside and see if I can reach down through the breech and pull it out," because it was like pounding against a rock. I got ahold of it and managed to pull it back through the breech and out of the gun. I put my head up to look down the barrel when "WHAM!" Someone pushed the rammer staff through and it hit me square on the nose.

I was introduced to the medics out there that day. It broke my nose and gave me two black eyes. I was a bloody mess when I came out of the tank. They said I looked like a stuck pig when I came out, the way I was bleeding. It hit me pretty hard, the brass end on that rammer staff. They took me over to the medics. I don't think the dispensary was fully set up yet. They set me in a chair and went to work with popsicle sticks up my nostrils to push things around and push my nose back into shape. They did a pretty good job because my nose is pretty straight. Sent me back to the motor pool and back to work with a butterfly bandage on my nose and told me to go to work. No time off. I was probably one of the first patients at that dispensary.

Long after the war, I got a phone call here one day.

"Vern," he says, "this is Snodgrass. Remember me?" He was my driver in the tank. This was probably within the last twenty years. He says, "I'm in Bellingham visiting my sister-in-law and her husband, and I just asked them if they knew you. They said, 'Yeah, if you look up the hill you can see Vernon's house.'"

A block away from me. First thing I knew he was walking up the hill here to come and see me. And he says, "Remember that incident on the desert when you got your nose broke and got cut up a little bit?"

"Yeah," I said, "I remember that."

"I was the guy running the rammer."

That was the first time I knew it. We got a big kick out of that.

Gill W. Terry, Headquarters Company, Recon Platoon. Interviewed 31 October 2003.

They shipped us to Bouse and put us on trucks and we drove and drove and drove. I said, "Where in the hell am I?" I didn't know where in the heck we were going and ended out in that Butler Valley and we got out there and there was nothing there. I remember the first night we were there, there were scorpions around and spiders and all kinds of stuff. They had some of those pyramidal tents up. But there was nothing around. I didn't know what the heck we were doing out there. I had no idea.

The way the army works, we were in Fort Knox—and I lived in Cleveland, Ohio, which was about 300 miles away—then they shipped us out to the desert and we got there in early September and were there two or three weeks and they gave us furloughs. So I had to come all the way from Phoenix all the way back to Cleveland. That's the way the army works. You would have thought they would have given the guys that lived in the east when they were in Kentucky a furlough then, and when they got out west, give the guys who lived out that way their furlough.

As I recall, they had a Lister bag hung up in the company street. A big bag on poles and they had that full of water. I found out later, of course, they had already built a reservoir out there and there was a well, Butler Well. The engineers who helped build the camp had already put that in. That's where the water came from.

A typical day depended on what we were doing out there. We were way beyond basic training at that time and everybody had their own little platoon that they were attached to. It depended on what they were going to do that day, whether assault guns, or in my case I was in a recon platoon. We did all our work at night. Slept during the day. We'd go out at night and sometimes we'd find our way around the desert by compass or else we'd go out and we'd play games like crawl around the desert and try to sneak through so-called enemy lines without being caught. Like you were on patrol. That was the idea, I guess. There were also the various rifle ranges; go out and shoot, either rifles, machine guns or whatever. And they had everybody qualify on most every weapon that was available.

As I recall, everybody out there had their own weapon and it was fully loaded. Everybody was walking around with live ammunition. M-1's, so-called .45 caliber grease guns, Thompson-type machine guns. They didn't have the drum magazine like Al Capone, just the long clip magazine. But everybody had live ammunition. That was kind of unusual.

But I don't recall, at least in our company, anybody getting hurt because of live ammunition. Every once in a while they would shoot some artillery over the top of your heads while you were sleeping in your tent just to get you used to it.

While I was out there, somehow I got assigned to "outpost guard." There were three entrances to that valley and they had guards on all three entrances to keep people in and out. We'd go out to these outposts and we'd be out there for two or three days. A couple days, anyway. I kind of liked it. Especially there was one way at the far eastern end of that valley. Alamo crossing. Way past Chocolate Drop. You'd go out there and you wouldn't see a soul. So it was great, you could do whatever you wanted. There were probably four or six of us. Just a few guys. You had the rations and would do your own cooking, do whatever you want. We had little stoves you could pump up and they would run on gasoline. We used to use GI gas. They were about the size of a coffee can. You'd pump them up. There was a little pressure thing and you could cook on those things. Everything out there in the desert was "B" rations. Pretty much dehydrated stuff. But at least in my case it was pretty potent because I gained weight eating that stuff.

I can remember they had these old army scout cars. They were something like a half-track. In the back we had machine guns up there. I can remember going out to Alamo Crossing—we'd be driving along and we'd take those machine guns and start shooting at jackrabbits with a .30 caliber while we were driving along.

I remember one time I was outpost guard at Cunningham Pass. That's the road that comes up out of Wenden. I was there one time and a big semi-truck came up and I don't know what he had in the truck, but we questioned him and I radioed it in and they said, "Bring him in." So I got in the cab with the guy and directed him in to the camp. I don't know why he came that way instead of the Bouse entrance, which was the main supply route into the camp.

There was always more traffic on that gate than there would have been any place else. Cunningham Pass and Alamo Crossing—there was hardly anybody coming. I really liked that—got away from all the baloney and politics at camp and all that stuff. There was always a lot of rumors flying around about what was going on and that type of thing, and of course some guys would get in fights over whatever for no particular reason and there was all kinds of pressure on the various officers.

Off duty, I didn't do very much. There were crap games and card games and they had a PX that served warm beer, when it was available. There wasn't a heck of a lot to do out there. I just stayed around the company area pretty much. We worked mostly at nighttime and slept all day. Everything was in reverse. They had some boxing matches between companies. As I recall there was a USO group that came out there, I think it was Kay Kyser. There were some female movie stars. The show was in that amphitheater, that depression in the ground.

When we first got out there it was so warm that you really couldn't work during the day: it was too hot. But later on, more towards winter, it got pretty darn cool at night. Sometimes you'd wake up in the morning and the water in the Lister bag in the company street would be frozen. No water until it warmed up a little bit. Then they had these little coal heaters in the center of the tents. They were pot-bellied stoves with the chimney going out the middle. It was built up on timbers with dirt in the middle and the stove set on that. Every once in a while they'd bring some coal and everybody would run for the coal and stock up to keep those heaters going.

It was hot and dusty and you just made do with what you could do. Sometimes you had to sleep out in the desert, not in the company area. You soon learned before you put a bed roll down to pound the ground all around where you were going to sleep because they had trap-door spiders that would come out of the ground. They always beat the ground before you lay down so you wouldn't get spiders and whatever else wild life that might be around. It didn't take long to learn to adapt to everything.

We always carried canteens with us and had a five-gallon can on a vehicle with you. When you came back from any job out there in the desert, the vehicles always had to be cleaned, especially the air filters because they were oil bath air filters and they would be filled up with dirt just from one day running around out there with all the dust. It's like the old cavalry with their horses; you had to take care of your horse before anything else. In this case, you had to take care of your vehicles before anything else.

Then we didn't get any passes for quite a long time. We did get a couple of passes to go into Phoenix—150 mile trip in a six-by-six on five-man passes. My wife and I were married in Phoenix, Arizona on a five-man pass. I knew I was going to have a three-day pass shortly before Christmas so I called Mary Lou, my fiancée, and said "Come on out here and we'll get married." When Sandy Rivchun was home on furlough back in late September, early October, he got married.

So Sandy's wife and Mary Lou came out to Phoenix on a train in December of '43. Mary Lou and I got married on the 27th of December, two days after Christmas, on a five-man pass. They rode the train all the way out to Phoenix. They stayed at a hotel for a while, they made the arrangements, got the church and the minister and everything else. I came in on the 27th and we got married that day. Sandy Rivchun was my best man. We stayed in the San Carlos Hotel and we got married and afterwards went to a steak house and of course I'm the last of the big spenders and everybody paid for their own meal. Walt Swinderman, he was in Headquarters Company also, he was the driver for the kitchen truck when they got overseas, and anyway, he was part of the wedding party, along with his mother. We went back to the hotel and got on the elevator and went up to whatever floor we were on, walked to our rooms, and that was that.

Then in the morning we came down to get breakfast and in Phoenix they had these CIC (Counter Intelligence Corps) people throughout the town and Mary Lou and I were sitting in the breakfast shop having breakfast and we were kind of nervous because we were just by ourselves. Nobody with us. We were supposed to have five men with us. I told Mary Lou, "See those guys over there? They're CIC." So she got all nervous, but they never did anything. Anyway, we got away with it. Everything worked out. Sandy's wife and Mary Lou got jobs out there and then they found a room in some house out on the edge of town. When we'd come in town, we'd come together, Sandy and I, and meet our wives and do whatever we did. When we found out we were going to go overseas, Sandy got the phone. He called and we told the girls, "Go to New York." We found out we were going to Camp Shanks somehow and told the girls, "Go to New York." So they went to New York and we met in New York at the Hotel Edison in New York City before we went overseas.

William C. Sweeney, Jr., Service Company.
Interviewed 20 November 2003.

The most I remember about the trip out to Camp Bouse is I pulled guard one day. We went through the tip of Texas, Amarill. I thought, "This is great"...for awhile. But you drag on for miles and all you see is level ground, so it got boring. But then when we got down...I guess the Arizona section of it, they had about three or four engines helping on the mountains. Even though it was Pullman cars for the troops, we also had flat cars for the tanks and trucks. We had taken our equipment and that's the reason they had three or four engines.

I remember when we got to Bouse. It seemed like we got there just before daylight and there were guys there with 6x6's to take us into the camp. I've always thought it was seventeen miles from Bouse where the depot was to the camp because I remember where the outpost was. They checked your tickets and you could see camp at that point, yet it was seven miles away to my remembrance. Out there the distance fools you completely. I know you could see the road going straight for ever so long then it made a complete L-shape, turned back to the left and in to the camp.

The temperature was something I wasn't used to. I believe they gave us a siesta from 11 in the morning till 2 in the afternoon for about two weeks until we adjusted to the heat. We got there in September. You're not used to that kind of heat but actually it didn't take long until you were adjusted to it.

The first time I drove a truck to get ammo in Needles, California, I opened the split windshield. Those trucks had a crank about the middle of the dash and you could crank them out about 4 to 5 inches. You would think that when you got out on the black top moving it would cool off but all there was is hot air. You learned just to crank the thing back in and stay cooped up because it wasn't fresh air, just hot air. Then you learned about the water bags. You'd hang that thing on the bumper of the truck and it would be covered up with dust because of evaporation. It would probably be caked on there a quarter inch or so but that water would be cool. And that tripod thing in camp with three legs on it, Lister bag fabric, rubberized fabric with spigots on it. I mean that was yuck, you know, because there was no cooling to it, just sitting out there in the dirt to drink from. But the water bag, that was a good deal. Of course you could freeze of the night, burn of the day. But you got used to it.

Once they gave us passes to LA. I went with Ray Harrison from Montana; we buddied together quite a bit. When we came back there had been a wash out, rain. Some of the outfits were tearing down the tents and my barracks bag was soaked about halfway through. Barracks bag was a draw string deal, bigger than a duffle bag, diameter-wise.

One of the things I'd do as truck driver, we took a double deck of gas cans in to the depot in Bouse. Overseas you haul triple deck which is 310 or 320 cans, five-gallon cans. This deal you'd haul only a double deck, take it out to Bouse and unload your empties. Then you waited until everybody got unloaded and loaded up with gas and head back to camp. Later the loading procedure was changed. We would disperse when loading; this would make us less of a target than bunched together. But sometimes a driver would fall asleep waiting and be left behind—better happening while training than in combat! Then you had to unload your gas to whatever company you were assigned to and then you had to service and fill your truck up. It was a forty-gallon tank and you didn't use too much on that trip, but you had to fill the forty-gallon tank, top it off. Then you'd take the oil bath air cleaner, which was what everything used for years and years till they went to the paper elements. You'd pour the oil out; pour some gas in, swish it around in the dark, moon light, whatever, you then had to guesstimate putting oil back in there up to the line. Then we'd raid the kitchen truck. It ran with the same convoy to get rations and bring them back to camp. And by that time we felt like having a snack, you know, so we'd have our snack with whatever the cooks fixed up for that day. We certainly didn't starve.

For the ammo there wasn't any bunkers. You just brought it in to the Tank Companies, "A," "B," or "C." I know the 75's that the tanks used were in round fiber containers and they were also in a triangle wood slat things too. The triangle was like a clover leaf, two stampings, with three shells in the triangle. They fit in those clover leaf things and there's a steel rod run through there to hold them together. Then they were cased up in a wood slat thing.

I witnessed a truck to blow up coming back from Needles one time, and I mean it left nothing of the truck. I was about the middle of the convoy with a guy from Akron as assistant driver. On each truck back then they'd have a sign. On the gas trucks you'd have red on a white background: "danger gasoline." They had the same thing if you had ammo: "danger high explosives." This particular time before we got to where we'd turn off the black top, I'm thinking, "Nothing ever happens." I'm thinking about these signs and following the truck in front of me and seeing the sign. Before we got to the outpost which is about seven miles...we were about eight miles from camp or so. And of course it was dusty. You ate dust all the time you traveled by vehicle. All of a sudden the truck in front of me stops and the driver drops out on his side and the guy on the other side gets out and runs away. I didn't see anything wrong and pull up in front of it.

What had happened was there were five bows on the truck. The idea was you used the canvas tarp when hauling personnel to keep them dry. But they had taken out four bows, leaving the one next to the cab in the pocket. He'd taken the tarp, rolled it up and tied to the bow. Well the tarp loosened up and dropped down between the truck cab and truck bed and caught fire on the mufflers. They got the fire extinguisher—each truck had one—but it wasn't enough. So here it was burning and I know the gas tank was on the right side. The convoy backed up and I don't know how far back they were. The ones in front of us knew nothing about it and continued on. I pulled up a little bit farther and I found myself—dummy me standing up on the cab of my truck—watching the thing take off. It was "sping, spow, bam, and boom." All of a sudden something came through the air like...like a boomerang or something, swish, swish, swish. I think it dropped pretty close to the back of the truck and I, I'm off there. I go up to the outpost and told them the truck just exploded ammo and all, but nobody was hurt.

To me there wasn't much to even look like a truck. You've got 75 mm and probably .50's and .30's on there. The gas that's on the truck, forty gallons, and you carried two five-gallon cans on the back of the truck at the mud guards. Anyway, it was a total, it was. That's just about the sum of that, nothing more to tell I guess, just one of those things. We lost one or two overseas by loose ammo or something. Nobody got killed, wounded or anything by it.

Editor's note: When the 740th Tank Battalion arrived at Bouse in mid-October, they saw the wreckage on their way to camp after getting off the train:

"It was not an enchanting scene, and if morale could have been measured with a conventional thermometer there would have been a minus sign in front of the figure. To make things a little worse, on the way into camp, the trucks passed the remains of an ammo truck. It had blown up and scattered duds for 200 yards in all directions. As the men passed by they wondered just how realistic the training they were getting into was going to be—whether this burned out truck was just the beginning."(Rubel, 1945, p.17)

The training was worthwhile for us. We were doing black-out driving and you got pretty proficient about it. You followed whoever led the convoy. Wherever they went that's where you went. One time somebody led the wrong way and we found ourselves on some of those mining roads. There were mines out there. On the vehicles were lights we called cat eyes, black-out lights. All the vehicles had these lights front and rear. Two little slots in each tail light so that's what you followed and wherever the lead person went that's where everybody else went, like a train. Wherever the leader went, you were in back of him. Overseas there were no lights so you had to do black-out driving.

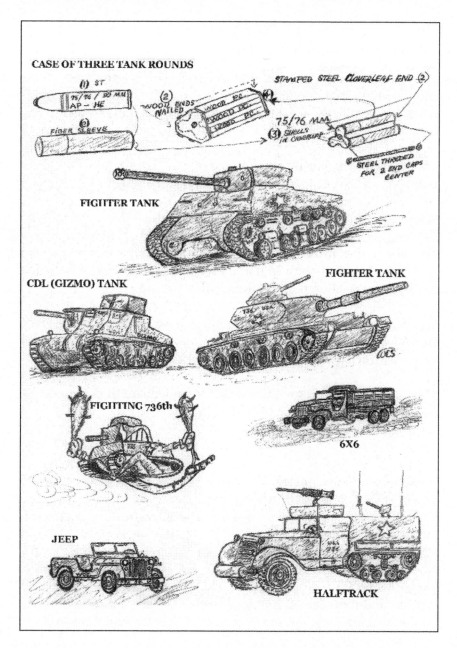

Illustrations by William C. Sweeney, Jr

Verne L. Brothers, "C" Company.
Interviewed 5 November 2003.

We worked mostly at night. We got to sleep in pretty good in the morning. Our night would end about two o'clock at night. We'd get up about eight in the morning. When we were off duty, we'd write letters, drink beer.... They had a sports thing going on. They had wrestling and boxing and you could join any of these you wanted to. They had a baseball team and I played on that. The captain was a football player. Each company had a football team and I played on that.

A few got out of line and the captain made them dig a 20 by 20 by 20. Until the priest saw it and he made him quit that. Father Mooney, he was from Notre Dame. He knew Newt Rockney real well and played football with him and everything. He was an interesting man. I went to church quite often, when I could.

Food was mostly canned. Not too much fresh stuff. When the army inspector came out he made them get more or less fresh stuff to go along with what we were eating. That was a good deal.

Of course I had to do my share of KP. KP and guard duty, those were the two main things.

They had passes going in to Phoenix on the weekends. You had to take your turn, of course. At Christmas time they had three-day passes going into L.A. I went with a guy—his brother was a sailor stationed in San Francisco. So we hitchhiked from L.A. up to Frisco. Halfway up there was a little town where his home was and we stopped and seen his mother, then we went on up to Frisco, saw his brother, went out all night and had a good time, and hitchhiked back in time to catch the trucks back to camp. In L.A. we went to the Paladium. Art Alexander was in there and he was dancing with some little girl about his size and they cleared the floor for them. They did real good. He was quite a jitterbug. He and Wireman were both from Canton.

We had buddy passes. At first there had to be four, with a sergeant in charge. If somebody started to talk about anything at camp you were supposed to knock him out and carry him back. It was ridiculous. That was what we was told, but nobody ever did anything.

There was one fellow in the desert, on Thursday, especially, he'd come around. I'd write my letters early and then I'd go to bed. Pete, the tank commander, was in the same tank I was. Him and his buddies would have a beer party in our tent. It was fine by me. I'd have a beer with them and then I'd go to bed. This guy, he always come around and give me a "piss call." I told him once, "I'm going to take you up there to the boxing ring and I'm going to put the gloves on and knock hell out of you." He was six foot two and I was five foot seven. He laughed and I said, "I'm going to do it the next time you give me a call." So he did and I took him up there and I got in a lucky punch all the way from the floor up to his chin and knocked him down and out for a few minutes. I took the gloves off and said "Now let that be a lesson to you." And I ran all the way back to the tent. He was a good fellow after that. He was quite a gambler. He'd been in and out of the big games. I understand he sent six thousand dollars home. He was either good or crooked. He was from Carolina, not Ohio.

Joseph F. Perrotti, Headquarters Company. Interviewed 27 October 2003.

There was nothin' there 'til we got there 'cause we had to put up our own tents, supply tent, kitchen, and latrines. The desert was really tough because we had no water. They just put a water tower up when we got there. We used to get a helmet full of water a day. No electricity. Everything was powdered. Powdered potatoes, no fresh meat or anything 'cause we couldn't refrigerate it. We had it maybe tougher in the desert than we had it when we went overseas, except they weren't shooting at us at Camp Bouse.

We were sort of amazed 'cause when you looked around, out of the camp, you had these cactuses and plants and stuff, but really it is beautiful, but it's blah. There's no buildings or nothing. All there was was land and mountains. You'd walk around in flour dough. There'd be no water in the river. If it did rain it would dry up before it even hit the ground almost. Everything was all sand. All sand. The wind blew and your tent got full of sand. When the wind blew and that sand come flying around it was no picnic because that stuff would cut your face. It was desolate. You get up the next day and it didn't change. It was the same thing. It was hot, but we weathered the storm.

We did our work at night because of the lights. We'd sleep during the day. Our days were all mixed up. We'd go out on bivouacs and problems and do little things we were supposed to be taught. An officer would take you out and would say, "We're going to do this and we're going to do that, we're going to attack this point and this is how we're going to do it." And then we'd try to do what the officer was saying. We just did what we had to do. We used to go on marches, different kinds of maneuvers, we'd engage in night fighting, and we learned how to take orders. We had to listen to these guys.

We were taught how in combat you had to do this and you had to do that. You listened to your superiors because this is the way we were going to do it. Just doing what they told you. At night you watched where your buddies were and if the officers said "advance" you'd advance. We weren't playing soldier; we were the soldiers. Next day you did the same thing until you got it through your head what they were trying to teach us. If you didn't watch out, if you did the wrong thing in combat, you'd die. You had to listen. You didn't say, "Well, I'm not going to listen to the guy." If you didn't do it right, you'd be dead.

Mostly there was repetitious things. You did the same thing over and over again 'cause they wanted to make sure you really knew what you were headed for. They were tough on us, but they wanted us to save a lot of lives. You had to watch what you were doing when you got close to combat.

We'd eat in the mess hall—well, there wasn't a mess hall. It was powdered this and powdered that. We used to get SOS—shit on a shingle—chipped beef gravy on bread. Like it or not, that's all you had. Except sometimes we'd give the truck driver—who'd be going in to town to get supplies—we'd give him a buck and he'd bring us back a dozen eggs and a loaf of bread. Instead of going to breakfast in the morning we'd fry the eggs right in our tent. We'd have eggs and bread, which was better than the powdered eggs at the kitchen. We were glad to give the guy a buck and we'd have a decent breakfast some time. Sometimes you didn't have a buck to give the guy, so you had to go to the kitchen to eat. When you ate that chipped beef as often as we were eating it, you disliked it real fast.

When we were not doin' anything we'd go into town, get soaked up, drink until we passed out. It didn't take much for me. When I was a kid I didn't go for drinking or anything. I didn't smoke until I got into the service. When I come out, it wasn't long after that that I quit. But we'd go into town and raise a lot of hell. Go to dances and stuff like that. Pick up a girl or something and go to a dance, but not too much else. And we got a lot of sleep sometimes.

Most of the time I was on KP or guard duty. When you were on guard duty, we had machine guns and you had orders to shoot if anybody came around. They had big gates across the little street we had. Those were the only ways to get in and out. We weren't getting out so we had to make sure that nobody was going to try and come in. It was just like being in combat. You had to be on your toes all the time. We had to go two hours on and four off. You had to watch. We had one lieutenant, Lt. Gochnour. When he was the officer of the day, we really had to be on our toes because at night he would come around and check to see if you were in a certain area and if you were doing what you were supposed to be doing. The other officers were sort of lenient. At night they didn't come and inspect us—they went to sleep. But Lt. Gochnour, he didn't go to sleep, he used to go to different places to see if we were doing our job. When he was on duty, you really watched yourself because he could be hiding behind one of the tents or behind the latrine or something and he'd jump at you to make sure you were alert.

When we got on the boat to go overseas he asked us, "Did you guys understand what I was trying to do?"

"Yeah," we says, "but we were going to throw you over the side of the ship; but we understood what you wanted and were trying to teach us." He was German himself, but he hated what the Germans were doing.

Jack W. Wireman, Service Company.
Interviewed 5 December 2003.

On the way out I remember being on guard in the turret of a tank. They made a stop at a crossing and cars were lined up on both sides. Of course you got off and walked and when I went back to get on the train I dropped my Tommy gun. I picked it up and threw it under a tank and got on about three tanks behind. I had to work my way back up to where the tank was to get the Tommy gun and get back in the turret. We went in rail yards at night, switching around and stuff. I wasn't out walking the post; I sat in the tank at night in the dark and you don't get out and roam around. That Tommy gun was loaded. It was one of the old regular Tommy guns with wooden handles.

I remember sleeping in the tank some and sitting in the turret when we were moving. They had to have relieved us; let us come back into a car of some kind during the time it took us to get out there. But most of the trip is more or less a blank.

To me, Camp Bouse was another sand pile. To tell you the truth, when they took us in on a truck it was all a new experience. You looked around and you saw sand, your tents, and the water tower. From then on you found out how it was to live out there in the sand pile. I've seen water freeze at night and by day time you better be out of your blankets. We slept with heavy comforters. By the time that old sun came up it really got hot out there.

I've brought tanks in off the desert or took them out to road test and you could take a cake of mud off, like a mask, off your face, when you removed your goggles. Your sweat just keeps pushing out against the dust that was flying and hitting you in the face. You could hold it in your hand; it was maybe anywhere from a quarter to maybe three eighths of an inch thick. That's one thing that amazed me. I had that happen a couple of times.

They had a tent to do the cooking in. You got food in your mess kit and then you hunted for a place in the sand to sit and eat. We kept our teeth pretty sharp on sand. When that wind blew up you'd get sand in your mess kit. We didn't have a building to eat in. We ate out in the open. Wasn't even any trees to lean against. We ate in the sand but it wasn't too bad. I liked to get up in the mornings and go get what they called "the shit on the shingles." Gravy, I'd get up every-day for that stuff. But as I remember we had pretty decent food.

They had boxing in the company, I guess—I never was much for that. I never went but to the group that came out. I couldn't tell you who they were. I guess a group from Hollywood. It wasn't one of the big names that I recall. I know we went up to a place where they showed movies at one time. You sat on benches and they enter-tained. I guess there was some singing and some dancing, I don't know what all.

748th was next to us on one side, down at the motor pool. I spent the biggest part of my time in the motor pool. We just had tanks and trucks come in to be worked on. We didn't work in a tent; we worked out in the open. We were really what you call too busy to think about what was going on. Back and forth to the motor pool and working on the tanks. We had training when we'd get up in the morning somewhere around…I think reveille was about two o'clock in the morning. At times we were on a sixteen or eighteen hour working shift and you had only a few hours off to sleep. I mean it was pretty strenuous sometimes.

We had the Gizmos then. They were training with them and we had a place out there that we called the stockade. I only went in there once or twice to work on the Gizmos. They were well protected. They were more or less locked up out there in what we called the stockade. I mean they weren't out roaming around till later on as far as I can remember. I was sent over one day to work on one that kept blowing the circuit breaker. The booster was the problem and I fixed it. Meanwhile my helper had the whole dash torn apart. I wasn't very happy so I told him, "You tore it apart, you got it to put back togeth-er again."

In a set up like that you have battalion maintenance, and each com-pany had their own maintenance. But when either couldn't take care of or when one got behind, the other maintenance would take care of it for them. We always had tanks down there to work on. With the Gizmos, there was a lot more to pull a motor out of one of them because of the big pulley on to the generator that made the light. As for any of the different things on the operation of it, I really don't recall. I knew how they could change the light from blue to yellow and flash it back and forth and stuff like that but I never saw any of that there. I don't recall seeing any of that stuff being worked, except when we were working on them or something like that.

I do remember the night I ran over 748's gas dump. I was lucky they were empty cans. I took a couple of guys for a ride on the desert. I "road tested" my tanks and when I took one out, I'd give them a good road test. A couple of the boys from the kitchen (and I don't recall their names now) wanted to go. We got out there pretty good, too far to get back before dark. When we got back all I could see was a row of lights down through there. I drove in and the next thing I know there was gas cans flying. I turned it around and went back out because I knew that wasn't my company. I was one group away. When we got in and parked the tank I told them guys to get going back to their kitchen. A jeep was already down there looking for a tank that had run through 748's gas dump. Until this day (and maybe I shouldn't tell this) but I am positive that Lieutenant Glindmeyer "knew" but he never said a word. I went to his tent and he asks me where I had been and I told him I had taken a tank out for a test run. He asked no more questions and they never did find out who ran over 748's gas dump. At least I didn't get penalized for it, anyhow.

There was fighter tanks out there. My first impression of that whole set up was, it wasn't feasible due to the simple fact that you had to have perfect terrain, perfect weather, and everything had to be practically perfect to make it blinding for the enemy. These tanks threw up a lot of dust so to me it was just a pipe dream really. We leave the desert out there and the next one we see is setting up on the river watching for mines. Well, I think we did work on some when we went overseas there in Wales in a rock quarry. But to tell you the honest truth, I never thought too much of it.

I don't remember being on KP out there at all. I remember drawing some guard duty, not too much company, and one time I did pull regimental guard. They took us way out in the desert to guard three ammunition dumps and I was on guard. We had passwords and you had to know the passwords, period. A jeep came in and I stopped it; I made the driver get out on one side and the officer on the other side. The officer was a Second Lieutenant, I think, but I had no idea who he was. He said he was the OD (Officer of the Day) so I told him, "Well, let's see your dog tags."

He went to bring them to me and I said, "You toss them to me."

While I'm questioning him I rolled his dog tags up so I could throw 'em back to him. He may still be trying to get that chain untangled. Then I answered his questions and gave him the information he wanted, he being the OD. Now ready to go, he wanted to know how to get to the other guards.

I said, "You have to go through here, but I can't let you through."

He says, "Well, how do I get up there?"

I said, "You don't. You don't know the password to get through here."

I had asked him for the password and he didn't know it. Well, he was gonna go through! He and the driver were sitting in the jeep not too far away from me. I threw a shell in the chamber and told him if they moved the first one went in the radiator and I didn't give a damn where the rest of them went. He told his driver let's get out of there and they left.

A short while later one of our second lieutenants in Service Company happened to be in regimental headquarters and heard about it. He said a lieutenant came in and he was still shaking, he was scared to death. When they were told what happened they wanted to know who that guard was out there. Our officer said, well that was one of the Service Company guards, his company. The OD asks him, "Would he have shot me?"

And he said, "I don't know."

He had to get out of there and go outside to laugh. He said, "I had an idea who it was." And he asked me, "Would you have shot him?"

I said, "You don't know either do you?"

He said, "And I never will, will I?"

I said, "No."

Eddie, if I'd let him through there, you know who's in trouble. I would have put the first one in the radiator. I don't know how many more I'd let go but I had a clip full in the carbine. But he took off the other way.

There were three ammo dumps if I'm not mistaken. But they had to go through the one where we were at. This was way out from the camp, and I mean you were out on the desert. I didn't see the other ones but I understood there was two more up there and there were guards up there too. They had to go through us to get there and if they didn't know the password and still got through, I could have been in the stockade. I never had one to do that and I never did find out who that officer was. He was probably from another outfit. That's the only time I pulled regimental guard.

When you're on guard duty you have to use a little sense. I was on guard at the stockade when Captain Allen came down one morning early to get one of his men in there, out. I told him, "Sorry, Captain, you can't get in there."

He said, "Well, I'm the OD!"

I said, "No, you're not the OD. When I came out on this post you weren't the OD."

Captain Allen had to go in and get the sergeant of the guard. I was the only guard they didn't tell who the new OD was when they changed. I remember when Captain Allen came out he looked at me and said, "Keep up the good work, sergeant," just like that.

We had to go on a twenty-seven-mile hike. I could walk and I had a fast gait. I started at the end of the column and after about the second break I was up and right on the lieutenant; he asks me to quit stepping on his heels. We slept out in the desert and I knew an old trick. I dug a shallow trench, put my bedroll in it, crawled in and covered it with sand. I slept warm as toast and when I got up that morning half them guys were froze to death. It got cold on that desert. They were making fun of me for burying my bedroll that night but I didn't pay any attention. I slept nice and warm and them poor devils was froze.

As I recall it was pretty near an all-day excursion hike, and then we were there overnight. They brought us food and stuff, fed us out there, and I think maybe they brought a mail call out to us. They took us back in trucks later on.

We did get a furlough. They took a bunch of guys to the train station and nobody had any money, period. One of the agents there in the railroad station called me into the office and asks how many tickets I needed. I told him it was five. He said, "I'll tell you what I'll do. If you give me your word that you will send the money—see that the money comes right back to me when you get home—I'll give you the five tickets. But if you don't send it back then I lose my job."

I remember that plain as day. I got home and the guys all give me the money and I mailed it back to him. That's the rough edges of it. I can't remember all the details. I do remember no money going home. I went to borrow some money off one of my buddies and he had two dollars and he give me one of them. I never ate so many doughnuts or drank so much coffee as I did on that trip going home.

Every time we'd get into a station we'd hunt the doughnuts. There were places at most stations that gave GI's coffee and doughnuts and sometimes it was sandwiches. I was on the train setting with a civilian. He had a bag lunch and offered me part of one of his sandwiches. I thanked him but didn't take it because I knew if I ate half of that sandwich them other four guys was gonna mob me when they had a chance. When we got home I sent the railroad agent his money and we now had money to get something to eat.

"Chet" Clapper, Service Company.
Interviewed 21 September 2002.

I drove truck in Service Company. We used to go in after gas and rations at night. A whole bunch of us would go in. They would shoot a flare off and we'd disperse. It was all blackout. I don't think we ever went in in daylight. It was always at night. For us to practice, 'cause once we got overseas, it was all blackout. We got the gas cans by the railroad tracks. American cans, not Jerry cans—the Jerry cans was just when we were overseas. It was all American five-gallon cans. The German [Jerry] cans were more like a square spout and ours was round.

They usually had the cans full. I don't think we ever had to fill 'em up. We'd just take empties in and get the full ones. Guys that was in there all the time, probably. I always went to Bouse. There might have been guys that went to Wendon, but I don't think so.

I didn't have to haul rocks there. Just gas and ammunition and stuff there.

One time two trucks passed other trucks and never knew it. It was unbelievable. A fellow by the name of Pasco, he went out in the desert and he kept on a goin' and never came back to the company for two days. He got lost out there. See, with a 6 x 6 truck, that goes through the sand pretty good. It was empty too, goin' in. We went in there pretty regular. It was so dusty. It was unbelievable. And blackout too. They couldn't see nothin'.

As far as training goes, we was on a twenty-five-mile road march out there, full field pack and one canteen of water. Everybody had to do it. Only once.

Another thing I had to do, a tank would run over you. You had so many minutes to dig a fox hole and a tank would run over you. In the sand, you had to dig pretty fast. That was one of the things I had to do. Them thirty-five-ton tanks. Had a little spade to dig with. You had so many minutes and had to dig pretty deep because the tank would go down in the sand pretty good. They went over everybody. Maybe some got away that didn't, I don't know.

Sometimes the tanks would be out on maneuvers and I'd have to take gas and ammunition and stuff out to them. A lot of times I'd take it out at night. They'd give me an azimuth reading and I'd have to haul it out to them. Blackout. Nobody with me.

Thomas G. Conaway, Headquarters Company. Interviewed 12 January 2004.

I thought it was all right. I was raised up and spent a lot of time in sagebrush country, not the cactus, but I thought it was OK. We had to have a twenty-five-mile walk before we were shipped out. Pete Henson, me, and it seems like one other hombre walked out twelve miles or so. We ate our K rations, took a little nap and when we woke up we could see our outfit disappearing in the distance headed back for camp. So we're wondering how we're gonna catch up with them and here comes a bunch of 748 trucks through. So we just crawled in the back of one of them and when we got to our outfit we stayed in the back of the truck. We rode into camp, took a shower, filled up our canteens with fresh water, and went out to the camp wash and waited for the returning guys that were walking. We felt sorry for them and blended in with the crowd while they were taking a break. The sergeant wanted to run the last quarter mile. Pete, the other hombre and I were hot for that. Man we showed him we were good soldiers, we were right up there. But don't tell the lieutenant.

Pete Henson and I one time took our sleeping bags and muskets and went out in the desert. We stayed overnight and shot a lot of ammunition just target practicing. It's cold out there in that desert; we found that out. But no, there wasn't much of anything to do, set around and listen to the boys play on their old guitars. We enjoyed that.

We had what was called "8 Ball." Somebody with a higher IQ than mine got "8 Ball" to drink water out of a canteen. So you're out there walking guard and it's dark. You hear a few footsteps and then something grabs you by the canteen. Believe you me, there's daylight under your feet. That's about the extent of the entertainment.

I can't think of anything I was doing. Burning a lot of ammunition. We'd go out there and shoot all we wanted too. I don't know what the duty was. I guarded "8 Ball." He had a habit of going over to the nurse's quarters and chewing their linen off the clothes line.

I remember one officer in particular, Lieutenant Gochnour. He was making soldiers out of us. He would get out there when we were on guard and take the gun away from us or something. But there were two of us he never did mess with. It was myself and a little jeep driver by the name of Ploe. I don't know why but he didn't mess with Ploe. The lieutenant mentioned something to me about "Don't let me take your gun away."

I said, "If you shoot somebody you get a transfer out of this place, don't you?"

He never did touch me and he really was a fine officer. All our officers were the best available, period. You couldn't ask for better officers and personnel. The only punishment I got, I had to eat that chow.

James H. Moon, "A" Company, 2nd Platoon. Interviewed 24 October 2003.

It was quite an experience getting out to Bouse. It was a passenger train but we only ate noon lunch on there. We'd just ride during the day time. At night they'd drop us off on a side track in some town. We'd eat; we'd go in a restaurant. We'd have breakfast there the next morning then we'd load back up on the train. The engine would come along and hook to us and carry us along. It took five or six days to go from Fort Knox, Kentucky to Phoenix, Arizona. We knew nothin' about where we were going or anything. Nobody would tell us anything. We'd ask but we didn't get no answers.

Once we hit Arizona our mail was censored. We could tell 'em we were somewheres in Arizona but we couldn't tell 'em where. When we went overseas we was not allowed to tell them anything that we were going overseas or anything. After we finally got overseas we could tell them we were overseas. But we couldn't tell them where we were.

I was with a bunch of replacements and we didn't learn [about the secret] until we got in the camp. I guess when they went through basic training they had a lot of men that they didn't think qualified.

We went in to replace those men. I went in this tank with Sergeant Storm, who was the tank commander. I can't remember the other men's names that was in the tank, right now, but I drove his tank and I stayed in his tank 'til we got to New York.

We got into Phoenix, Arizona early in the morning and we spent the day in Phoenix. We had no idea. They woudn't tell us anything about where we were going. Late that evening they loaded us back up on the train and we headed west again; we still had no idea where we were going.

About nine o'clock, the train just stopped. We unloaded with all our equipment, our duffle bags and everything, there on the side of the train track. We set there and waited; not a building, no lights or anything in sight. After a while we saw some headlights way out in the desert coming towards us. They got there and it was GI trucks coming to pick us up. We loaded on to those trucks and started across the desert, still no idea of where we were going.

We topped this hill and we saw all of these lights. We could tell it wasn't buildings. And our hearts just sank. It was tent city. We got into camp and part of the men were on furlough. This was in December, just a few days before Christmas. They didn't come back into camp until after Christmas. The first thing they told us when we were briefed that night, that no one would get a furlough. The unit was alerted to go overseas and there would not be time for us to have a furlough. We stayed four months before we went overseas. Nobody got a furlough.

I guess it was the first night when we got in the camp, most of the boys was on furlough but they were still a lot of them in camp. About midnight they got out and opened up with .50 and .30 caliber machine guns. They was firing everywhere and we were scared to death. We had just come in and weren't used to no such as that. We got under our cots—we were sleeping on little ol' cots—tried to get under our cots for protection. We were scared to death. I don't know whether they ever caught the boys that was doin' it or not, but they was just firing all over them camps. Just comin' out of basic training, you didn't know what was going to happen.

I hear men talking now about what sorry food they had but I guess we had unusual good cooks. They could take those C rations—we had C rations even when we were in the desert—and they could make them taste pretty good. We were fortunate that we had some pretty good cooks. We had a lot of pancakes. They were delicious. I thought they were, anyway. Didn't have no fresh vegetables, just all canned vegetables.

We had five-man tents. The tank crew lived in one tent. You had showers out in the open. They had pipes strung across the end of the tent row and that's where you'd get your showers. They had some little curtains hung up to half-way protect you from being seen by someone else. The tents had a little pot-bellied stove in the center where you could have a little fire.

I had one pass while I was there. We had to go on buddy passes. I believe it was six that had to be together. We had to stay together. We had our own MP's in town, and if we got separated our MP's would pick us up and put us in jail. We had quite a few of them that got put in jail while we were there. With the buddy passes you were not allowed to separate, you were not allowed to talk, you were not allowed to say anything about where you were stationed or anything.

They never did debrief us and tell us that we were free to talk about it. So it was a long time that you never heard it mentioned when we would go to our reunions. They wouldn't mention it too much. We had been taught to be so secretive about it that the men just still stuck to that.

I was very depressed when I got in the desert and the message that we'd not get furloughs. It didn't last long. After I met a few of the guys and got acquainted with them and got involved in going to the show and whatnot out there—wasn't too much we could do out there in the desert. We did have a movie, though. It was real interesting; we'd go to the movie. We had an open-air theatre. They had a big screen down in front.

See, I was born in the South where it was warm and not too cold anytime. But in December, we'd go to the movie in our shirtsleeves but we'd carry our overcoats with us. By the time the movie was over it would be so cold we'd have to wear our overcoats back to the camp. One show I remember seeing out there was Kay Kyser. He put on a show there for us. He was in person. It wasn't a movie. I don't remember any of the movies I saw there.

Our training went so swift we had to adapt pretty fast to what we were doing out there. All of my training was done at night. We'd sleep during the daytime. The training—about the main thing I remember about the training was when we had to learn to crawl under fire. We had a course there that was about 100 feet long, maybe 200 feet, and we had to crawl across that space under .30 calibre machine gun fire. Live fire over you. I can remember the night we had that I had bumped my knee on the turret of the tank and I had a terribly sore knee and I couldn't hardly walk. But I went through that field course. I was the last one to get through with it and I was hurting so bad I couldn't even crawl. I thought I never would get through there. But I finally made it through it. I passed it. You'd crawl over logs and down into little ditches and be careful when you come out that you didn't get your head up too high. It scared us to death. I don't know how low them bullets were but they were going over the top of us.

I can remember the searchlights, seeing the searchlights for the first time on the tanks. I was amazed at what they did. They were bright. They would blind anything that was out there. I remember as we were training, the infantry would be in between us, there would be movement out in front of us. I can remember, too, seeing jackrabbits. We'd see jackrabbits when we'd shine those lights. I can remember seeing them big ol' jackrabbits out there. And cactuses. You had a lot of cactuses standing up. They looked like people and they just cut them off with machine guns.

I can't remember too much of the inside of the Gizmo. After we went overseas we never did get back inside the Gizmo. We had 'em in Wales and we had 'em until we went over into France. As we got into France, we got regular tanks. We were still considered part of the Gizmos and we've always said that that's what kept us from going to the front lines before we did. We didn't go into combat until ten days after the invasion. They were in a hundred miles then and we set up in an apple orchard and set there for four months.

I never did dig a foxhole as long as I was in the army. I remember sitting on the front lines in the first combat we had, and the infantry would dig in out in front of us. It was in the winter time and they wouldn't any more get there and again we'd move up, but wouldn't move up more than fifteeen or twenty feet. And they'd just have to go through diggin' again. I felt so sorry for those infantrymen out there. Ground frozen and trying to dig a foxhole. I was just thankful that I wasn't drafted into the infantry.

We came out of the Gizmos and went into regular tanks. Our first day of combat was one of the worst we had the whole time we were over there. And I can't remember to save my soul loading that gun while we were there. But I know I loaded it and I know we fired it. But I can't remember the details. I know when I went into combat I was horrified because if something happened and I'd had to tear that gun down inside that tank I don't know what I would have done. I was taught and thought I knew pretty well about tearing it down if something happened to it, but I was still scared and didn't know if I could do it or not. But I was thankful that nothing happened that I had to tear it down.

Jack D. Gay, Headquarters Company.
Interviewed 22 December 2003.
Supplemented with excerpts from Jack's own family history.

I joined the 736th Tank Battalion the second week of January 1944. A steam engine picked up our railroad car at Fort Knox and we were added to a passenger train in Louisville. There were about forty to fifty GI's in the car, all privates. To everyone's surprise there was a lieutenant colonel setting in a seat with a big stack of papers stuffed into a briefcase on the seat beside him. He told us he was temporarily in command and would be until we reached our destination. I was very impressed with how sharp he looked in his uniform. He looked out of place and stood out like a sore thumb among all of us rookies. He was a good looking man who stood about six foot two with salt-and-pepper hair and a mustache, built like a professional football player. To us eighteen and nineteen-year-olds, he looked old enough to be our father. Nowhere on his uniform were there any patches to identify what kind of outfit he was with or what branch of the army he was serving...

Here are some excerpts from my first letter home which I started after leaving Fort Knox.

> Monday: Your son is on a train heading west and we are now passing through St. Louis. I won't be able to mail this until we arrive at our destination....We had a good meal at noon, cream of chicken.

> We are allowed a $1.00 meal allowance....We left Ft. Knox at 4:30 this morning....

> Tuesday: We are now in Kansas City. Just finished breakfast. Both St. Louis and the Kansas City railroad stations have restaurants for GI's only. KC has more tracks at its station than I've ever seen, 35! ....The cities in the mid-west sure are dirty, St. Louis the worst of all....These sleepers are pretty nice, only woke up once during the night when I had a bad coughing spell. I rubbed some of the Vicks you sent me and I also swallowed some like you taught me. My cold seems much better this morning.

> I can't understand how most of my buddies got so much money given them while they were home. Ralph Murdica's friends gave him $100 and another got $25.

> Wednesday: We just went through a very beautiful part of the country, the Rocky Mountains. We are now in New Mexico.
>
> Thursday: It looks as though the west would be a nice place to live. We had supper in Albuquerque and were served a steak dinner at Fred Harvey's. I was told that they have them all over the west. It was swell. All towns out here are nice and clean and the people!!

(1/4 of the page was cut off at the bottom by a censor. Yes, all my letters were checked out by our officers while we were in the States from this point on).

I ended the letter with the following:

> Saturday night: We finally arrived at our destination and it's not as bad as I thought it would be. From now on my style of writing will have to change. Don't worry, there's not much I can tell you and a lot of questions you would like to ask I can't answer. If you think it's time to send a box of goodies, throw in some candles. I hope it will be one of those world famous boxes like you sent me while we were in battle training at Knox. It will sure sound good when I hear the name "Gay" at mail call for the first time since I arrived at this station. (Gay, 1998, p.4)

We arrived at our destination shortly after midnight the next day. That night was pitch black and you could make out a small railroad station, a house or two, and three or four army trucks standing by to take us somewhere on an unknown desert. We boarded the trucks and sat on the bench-type seats. Before leaving the station, a canvas was pulled over the entrance to the truck bed. It did help a little with the dust the convoy made as it traveled the gravel road across the desert, but we couldn't see anything and that made us a little nervous.

About twenty minutes on a road we started going up a grade and soon the convoy came to a halt. We were told to dismount and fall in beside the truck. As I left the truck, I couldn't help but notice a tower with a 30-cal. machine gun along with a 50-cal. machine gun on a half-track pointed in our direction, manned by serious-looking soldiers.

The orders were turned over to our welcome committee by the lieutenant colonel and he left in a jeep heading back.

The next thing was to take an inventory. As our names were called we took a couple of steps forward and gave the person in charge our dog tags so he could verify who we were and if they matched the names and serial numbers on our orders. By that time we were so tired from our travels that we didn't think about all the special attention. I thought, "Let's get it over with and get some sleep!"

After driving down from the pass to the desert floor, we finally reached our destination and still didn't know much about our situation. We were then escorted to our assigned battalion. About five or six of us went to the 736th Tank Battalion (Special). We were led to a tent, told to get a good night's sleep and that we would be quarantined in our tent from the others in the battalion until some time the next morning when we were to receive an orientation. After about four hours sleep, we were awakened and escorted to breakfast by an armed guard. This time I'm really wondering what the heck I'm getting into.

After breakfast we returned to quarters and we were sitting on our cots when the major walked in followed by several subordinate officers. We quickly called ourselves to attention and just as fast the major barked back, "At ease men, as you were. It's alright for you to remain where you are while I speak to you. I'm Major George P. Callison and I want to convey to you your situation." Some of the information he gave us at that point was:

- We were in the 736th Tank Battalion, Special, located at Camp Bouse, Arizona
- The "Special" indicated that it was not a regular tank outfit
- Our tanks were to be used in night fighting
- The tanks were old M-3's (General Lee)
- The 37 mm cannon in the turret was replaced with an arc light
- Because of the nature of the secret project, our outgoing mail would be censored
- When we received a weekend pass, there would be at least two

and sometimes as many as six GI's on one pass

I must admit, it felt kind of special to be a part of a "secret" outfit. And the opportunity to work and explore the Mojave Desert seemed appealing to me also. I was assigned to the reconnaissance platoon in Headquarters Company, an adventurous sounding name to an eighteen-year-old rookie like me. (Gay, "Replacements for Camp Bouse, January 1944," in Maddox and Maddox, Jr., editors, 1997).

Most training began at 1500 hours (3 p.m.) and would take most of the night, since the Gizmo was a nighttime weapon. It was aimed at perfecting small unit operations, with heavy emphasis on platoon teamwork, supporting fire, time on target, and split second maneuvering — with the goal that it became second nature. Weapons cross training was begun, and soon tank repairmen were handling mortars like professionals. To further this standardization and to help realistic combat training, a small cadre of British officers was assigned to Camp Bouse shortly before its closure.

Other combat techniques were used to make our training more realistic. This included night artillery fired directly over the camp with minimum clearance. This was done on a nightly basis so those who were having a rare evening for relaxation would not forget what they were training for. Sleep was hard to come by, but the troops adjusted.

By day it was maintenance. By night it was practice, practice, practice. The object was to keep ten to fifteen tanks lined up abreast with a ninety-foot separation between them. Armored infantry would move up into the "Cone of Darkness" of two CDL's. In combat, Sherman M-4 tanks would be added to some of these cones. This force would be invisble (to the enemy). With their machine guns blazing and their 13 million candlepower arc lamps turning night into day, the tanks would attack various simulated targets in the valley late at night. One of our favorites seemed to be a small hill in the middle of the valley which we named "Chocolate Drop" because of its resemblance to the candy. From over twenty miles away, their arc lamps caused a reflection in the sky resembling an aurora borealis gone mad. A dozen or so Gizmos would illuminate a vast area and make it stage-like. It was exciting for those of us in support troops to be able to be near a radio and hear the task force commander give the commands to the arc light operators as they moved forward.

To turn the lights on: "Prepare to Heat, Heat now," or "Prepare to Halo, Halo now"; to use the color filters: "Prepare to Rainbow, Rainbow now"; to use the flicker device: "Prepare to Scatter, Scatter now." It was not the weapon but the strategy involved which was the greatest secret. If we could surprise the enemy at night and light up his position, we could have all the advantage of a playgoer in the audience. Our mission was to develop a technique, perfect it, and take it into battle. (Gay, 1998, p.4)

We did a lot of our work at night. We'd come in in the mornings and have breakfast and sleep until noon and then be off a couple of hours, then we'd get ready for the night stuff.

It was kind of a shock to learn, when we'd go on these maneuvers, what our mission in recon was—to be out in front of the tanks and locate them and radio back where they were and that type of thing. I thought "Boy, we're really in a dangerous position!"

Off duty, one of the most fun things, I guess you would call it, that we did—a friend of mine who trained with me at Knox was in another battalion. This clip from one of my letters describes what we did:

> February 2, 1944. I really had an interesting fun day, probably the best since entering service. Ralph Murdica, one of the boys I took basic training with, and I got a .22 rifle and some shells from his company and went hunting. We had plenty of ammunition, and if there was any game around we probably scared it off as we shot at everything.

And in another letter I mention going to church:

> February 6, Sunday. I got up early and took myself to church.
> The Chaplain was very interesting as he condenses his sermons
> like the stories in the Reader's Digest. His sermon was on Baptism.
> This church service was the first Sunday I was off quarantine and
> I was looking for something to do. I wrote my mother about it,
> and he also wrote a nice letter telling about me and I still have
> that letter.

(Note: Jack sent a copy of the letter, which follows on page 183.)

V. L. WUNNEBURGER. Chaplain
Headquarters Ninth Tank Group
APO 188   % Postmaster
LOS ANGELES, CALIFORNIA

February 8, 1944

Rev. Gairson
Kanawha City Presbyterian Church
Charleston 4, W. Va.

Dear Rev. Gairson:

It was a joy to have had the privilege of
greeting our mutual friend, Pvt. Jack D. Gay,
in our service in the beautiful Cactus Chapel. I
cannot help but think of the words of Queen
Elizabeth of England, in an Empire-wide broadcast:
"I would like to add with my fullest conviction
that it is on the strength of our spiritual life
that the right rebuilding of our national life
depends. In these last tragic years many have
found in religion the source and mainspring of
courage and selflessness that they need."

I am happy that we have this member of your
church in our command and I want you to know of the
satisfaction we have in having him in our services,
and in his friendly attitude that gives us this
privilege of advising you that while he is in this
camp, he makes the chapel a port of call in these
times of storm. His name is not only on our registry
but he and his family, and friends as well as his
comrades in arms, will be in our prayers until these
 troubled days are past.

It will be a blessing to hear from you at any
time.

Very cordially yours

V. L. WUNNEBURGER
Group Chaplain

That same day I wrote about a USO show we had.

> An announcement on bulletin board said Kay Kaiser and a group
> of actors, singers, and dancers, along with his band, were going to
> put on a show, and what a show it was, the best I've ever seen.
> He was master of ceremony. Marilyn Maxwell was the lead singer.
> She was a star in the movie, "Salute to the Marines," with
> Wallace Berry along with Paramount actress, singer and dancer,
> Katherine Fike. Both were blondes and the guys went crazy as you
> don't find many blonde girls out here in the desert. Other stars were
> Jack Haley, I'm sure you know him, and Jim Burke. He always plays
> the part of an Irish policeman or an Irish character. Those were the
> big names I remember, but there were others that gave us a good
> show. There was a comedian singer, a girl ventriloquist who is on
> the Eddie Cantor radio show and another male dancer. There were
> others involved and they gave us a good show. The jokes were nasty
> at times, but I guess that helped to make the show so great.
> (Gay, n.d., p.71; Gay, 1998, pp.4-5)

Other excerpts from Jack's letters to his mother reflect more of the
entertaining side of life.

> February 14: We had a big sandstorm over the weekend.
> Everything in our tents was covered....I had a very enjoyable
> couple of days in Phoenix. We were transported in a convoy by
> the US Army. This helped with the cost. Some of us had a
> hard time finding lodging. We finally got one in a private
> home through the Servicemen's Center. It was in a ritzier part of
> town. The lady of the house wouldn't accept any money from
> us and said it was a part she could play in helping out with
> the war effort.
>
> I spent most of the time eating and dancing with girls my
> age at a Servicemen's Club in the basement of a Catholic Church.
>
> February 16: Just got back from a USO show and it was pretty
> good. Mrs. Edward G. Robinson brought the show here
> from Los Angeles. All the entertainment and boxing events are
> held in a nice outdoor theater.
>
> March 9: The box of goodies you sent is going fast. The cookies
> went the first night. I'm making use of the last jar of jam.

Each box you send is always bigger and better than the last one.
The socks and candles are just what I needed. THANKS!

March 21: I really had a swell time on a three day pass to
Los Angeles where we spent most of our time in Hollywood.
We had a hotel in the middle of everything, just a walk of three
blocks to Radio City or the Brown Derby. I saw a lot of movie
stars at the Hollywood Canteen and I had a little chat with
Lloyd Nolen when he served me a sandwich at the food bar.
(Gay, 1998, p.5)

The "Kid Battalion" had a lot of guys like me who did not have a
girlfriend or wife to receive letters and goodie boxes at mail call. We
would all gather around company headquarters, and as our names
were called and we were handed a package you knew that there
would be a bunch of guys at your tent to help you open it, and hope
there would be food to share. In our company, I would vote for Joe
Perrotti's mother as the Queen of Goodie Boxes. She introduced me
to one of the best snacks that I had ever had: pepperoni!

Another popular pastime during the day, before our work at night,
was to put on boxing gloves with one of your buddies. The battalion
had a ring at the end of one of the company streets and it was used
quite frequently. Before I arrived at Bouse, boxing events between
companies and battalions were held in the area where we were
entertained by the USO. Also, I remember sparring a few rounds
with Gilbert Garcia who had some Golden Gloves experience in Los
Angeles before entering service. I learned not to be too good, as
every time I got a good lick in, he would give me back two better
ones! (Gay, 1998, p.5)

I was a pretty good boxer. At home there was a Polish family that in
their basement, the oldest brother trained the other brothers to be
boxers and they were all in the golden gloves and that sort of thing.
And they worked with me. (At Bouse) in spare time, when we weren't
going on leave or anything like that, we would box. My problem
was, if I got a lick in, and these guys had the experience, man, you
had to really watch and not hurt them, because if you hurt them,
they were going to get you.

Gilbert Garcia, Headquarters Company.
Interviewed 11 November 2003.

Camp Bouse? Hell, it was hell. That's where I did my boxing there in Bouse, but it was hell. They used to take us to a hill they called Chocolate Drop. They would take us out there for training. There was a lot of cholla cactus. I remember one time in a jeep I had that windshield down and we hit a cholla cactus. It hit me right on the knee, it stuck there and man I tell you…those stickers had to be pulled out with pliers. But we were young and we could take it. I couldn't take that kind of weather now. I heard that a lot couldn't take it but some of us were used to hot weather, California is close to Arizona. A lot of the boys that came from cold weather, well it was kind of hard for them.

They would say when you're walking and you hear a rattle, stop and walk the opposite way, just don't look for the snake. We used to go out for a hike to keep our legs in good shape, that's what I would say anyway.

We had a real good first sergeant; he used to go right with us. Sergeant Chuck McCarthy. He's a big guy. He used to say "just give me the boys from East L.A., you can have the rest." They took us on a hike one time; I was in his platoon, an assault gun platoon. He'd get us to start singing Rancho Grande or something just to keep morale up. You never heard that man cuss a bad word.

At one time I was driving a jeep for Lt. Gochnour, one of the officers. I drove for him quite a while but then I was transferred to an assault gun platoon and drove a halftrack. I remember one time in Europe we were sitting in the halftrack and Sgt. McCarthy was asleep in the back. There were shells dropping and they kept getting nearer and nearer. I woke him up and he said, "Oh Gil, just move up a little ways and the shells won't get us. You messed me out of a good dream, I was dreaming of a big steak in New York."

Camp food was all right, I'm a good eater. It didn't bother me that they would throw the food right on your mess kit as you went by. But you know, compared to overseas it was good. Over there you got little "K" rations.

There was no entertainment. Guys did get out there with their guitars and sing, that's about it. There was nothing entertaining in Bouse except the PX where you go get a couple of beers, the boxing, or getting out there with their guitars.

Nobody could leave unless you went supervised. We would leave Camp Bouse and go to Phoenix or Glendale, Arizona but we had to be in a group, we could not go by ourselves. If anybody started to open their mouth the other guys would tell them to shut up. We would go down to Glendale where they used to have teenage dancing. That's another thing I love to do, dance.

Just before we left for overseas I got a ten day furlough. Ten days out of the three years. That's when I got my five fights. I got to meet James Frankenberg and Ingrid Bergman.The movie stars were waiting on us, they were really nice. I was in Hollywood and because it was so close to East L.A. I snuck out of the Palladium and I went home for a couple of hours then I went back again. I got a cab and went out to East L.A. from Hollywood. Hollywood is only about six miles from East L.A.

Lt. Coveney tried to catch Ramon and me…We used to sneak out of the camp. We would wait for one of the guys from East L.A. to be on duty at the motor pool. We'd go get a jeep and disconnect the speedometer. They used to say nobody can get out of Camp Bouse. We would get out and get back in.

We'd go down to a night club in Parker. Four or five of us would go down, have a few drinks and do some dancing, stuff like that, and then come back. That was our mean thing we used to do.

We didn't go too often. There was a bridge out there and they blew it up. They said nobody could get out now that they had blown the bridge. But we used to get the jeep and go over beside of the bridge on the hill. The guys would hang on to the side of the jeep so it wouldn't flip over to get to the other side.

You know...the way we looked at it...we were going to war in Europe. We better have a good time before we go.

Another time when we were at Camp Bouse we went down to Pomona to a depot where they have vehicles and there were a couple of trucks that got blown up or something. I was there with about six or seven guys and a warrant officer. We went down to Pomona to get trucks and jeeps and bring them back to Camp Bouse. I told the warrant officer, "You know, I only live ten or fifteen miles from here. Why don't you let me go home?" We weren't going to go back to Arizona until tomorrow.

He said, "I can't do that, I can't do that." I was really heart broken because I was so close and yet so far. But in the morning he said, "Garcia, we're going to go down to your mother's house." As I got off, all these guys start getting off of the truck. I tell you my mother couldn't believe it. The guys went into the house. We had a neighborhood store about four houses from my house and the man...well he knew me since I was a kid. He brought a bunch of meat and fruit and everything to feed the guys. So my mama went in to prepare the food.

I remember Eddie Piper. He was from Maine and he bit into an avocado. I said, "Eddie, you don't eat an avocado that way."

He said, "I don't like it."

I said, "You don't eat it that way, you make guacamole and get a little salsa and it goes with it."

I thanked that warrant officer for bringing me home. We all went, we all ate and we all left. There must have been, I'd say, between six and eight guys and the warrant officer because we had to exchange drivers. Driving for a couple of hours at 30 of 35 miles an hour, you had to keep a certain distance from the guy in front of you...military you know. You would get tired so the front truck would park and you would change drivers.

But my mama had to make a big meal that day, she made a lot of food and everybody ate.

I remember when I came home, one of my cousins that was a little bit older than me...grabbed me from the back. I grabbed him by the head and flipped him on his back. He said, "They taught you something in the Army." My brother was always picking on me when I was a kid. We put on the gloves, my dad moved all the furniture out of the way in the living room and my brother and I went at it with the gloves. He said, "Kid, you learned something." But not only that, the Army taught me...not that I didn't know how to respect people but to, you know, to look up to people. You just don't pick at people or anything like that. I learned how to be a better man I would say, because I have been married to my wife for 57 years.

Jesse R. "Pete" Henson, Headquarters Company
Interviewed 19, 20 June 2002

3.2 percent was the strength of the beer. That was all you could get. Our donkey, "8-ball," liked that beer too. He'd come right in the tent with us and we'd put a helmet down and pour a bottle of beer in it and he'd drink it. On occasion he got tipsy. He'd trip on his feet and start to bray and wheeze like he had bad lungs. Quite a comedian.

That's how our donkey got in trouble. He went in one day when the nurses were all on duty. The guard didn't shut the gate, he just stood there by it. Our pet donkey had the run of the camp. He was curious and ambled by the guard and the jackass proceeded to eat up the nurses undies that were hanging on the line. One of the girls was screaming and crying to the colonel. He was an old reprobate— thought he was a ladies' man—Col. Bill Dodge, "Wild Bill Dodge" he called himself. He got in his jeep and whipped out his trusty .45 and went up and caught "8-ball" and just emptied his magazine into his guts. He didn't try to kill him, he just gut-shot him. The donkey layed there wheezing and the colonel drove off. A sergeant got his carbine and killed the poor beast. We loaded him on a truck and buried him.

The End

References

701st Tank Battalion. Ed. Edward C. Hassett. Nurnberg, Germany: Sebaldus-Verlag, 1945.

Baty, Roger M. "Arthur L. Alexander. Oral History Interview," Cherry Valley, California, 12 November; 25 November 2002.

---. "Chalmer Chester (Chet) Clapper. Oral History Interview," Warner Robins, Georgia, 18 - 22 September 2002.

---. "Clayton A. Helgeson. Oral History Interview," Seattle, Washington, 13 September 2003.

---. "Gill W. Terry. Oral History Interview," recorded from Redlands, California, 31 October 2003.

---. "Jack D. Gay. Oral History Interview," recorded from Redlands, California, 22 December 2003.

---. "James H. Moon. Oral History Interview," recorded from Redlands, California, 24 October 2003.

---. "Jesse R. (Pete) Henson. Oral History Interview," Wenden, Arizona, 19,20 June 2002.

---. "John Mellon. Oral History Interview," Warner Robins, Georgia, 27 September, revised by John Mellon 11 October 2002.

---. "Joseph F. Perrotti. Oral History Interview," recorded from Redlands, California, 27 October 2003.

---. "Otera V. Coffman. Oral History Interview," recorded from Redlands, California, 13 October 2003.

---. "Robert V. Olsen. Oral History Interview," Seattle, Washington, 12 September 2003.

---. "Verne L. Brothers. Oral History Interview," recorded from Redlands, California, 5 November 2003.

---. "Vernon Tweit. Oral History Interview," recorded from Redlands, California, 10 October 2003.

Bischoff, Matt C. *The Desert Training Center/California-Arizona Maneuver Area, 1942-1944. Historical and Archaeological Contexts.* Tucson, Arizona: Statistical Research, Inc., 2000.

Blanchard, W. J. *Our Liberators: The Combat History of the 746th Tank Battalion During World War II.* Tucson, Arizona: Fenestra Books, 2003.

Daniels, Stuart L. "The Mystery of Our Most Secret Weapon." *The American Weekly* [Cleveland Plain Dealer] 11 August 1957: 18-21.

Denning Sr, Carsie. phone conversations and e-mailings. 24 June 03 through 11 March 04 2003,2004.

Gander, Terry J. *Tanks in Detail: Medium Tank M3 to M3A5.* Bournemouth, Dorset, England: JSS Publishing Limited, 2003.

Gay, Jack. "The 736th Medium Tank Battalion (Special) Fort Knox, Camp Bouse, Wales, Northern France and Its Secret," 27 August 1998.
---."The War Years." *The Gay Family Story*, n.d. 63-86.

Henson, Jesse R. "Pete." "My War," 1991.

Hunnicutt, R. P. *Sherman: A History of the American Medium Tank.* Belmont, California: PublishersPress, 1978.

James, A. "Death Rays in the Preselis—Secrets of World War Two—American Gizmos and the Candle Light Caper." *Pembrokeshire Life* 1999.

Johnson, Mike. "Camp Bouse: Desert Training Center, California/Arizona Maneuver Area." Published by the Lost Dutchman, Billy Holcomb, and John P. Squibob Chapters of the Ancient and Honorable Order of E Clampus Vitus. Bouse, Arizona, 17, 18, 19 January 1997.

Kennedy, John W., John S. Lynch, and Robert L. Wooley. *Patton's Desert Training Center*. Fort Myer, Virginia: Council on America's Military Past, 1st revision, 1986. No.47, Journal of the Council on America's Military Past, December, 1982.

Maddox Jr, Eddie L. "Gilbert Garcia. Oral History Interview," recorded from Franklin, Georgia, 11 November 2003.
---. "Grady Curtis Gaston. Oral History Interview," recorded from Franklin, Georgia, 13 January 2004.
---. "Jack W. Wireman. Oral History Interview," recorded from Franklin, Georgia, 5 December 2003.
---. "Robert S. Lamneck. Oral History Interview," recorded from Franklin, Georgia, 13 January 2004.

---. "Thomas G. Conaway. Oral History Interview," recorded from Franklin, Georgia, 12 January 2004.

---. "William C. Sweeney Jr. Oral History Interview," recorded from Franklin, Georgia, 20 November 2003.

Maddox Sr, Eddie L., and Eddie L. Maddox Jr. *736 Special Tank Battalion: Thoughts and Memories from the Men of the 736th.* Blankenship & Walker Printing Co., Inc.; Forest Park, Georgia: Eddie L. Maddox Senior, 1997.

Meller, Sgt. Sidney L. *The Desert Training Center and CAMA.* Study No. 15, Historical Section—Army Ground Forces. 1946.

Rubel, Kenneth George. *Daredevil Tankers: The Story of the 740th Tank Battalion United States Army. Gottingen, Germany:* Muster-Schmidt, Ltd., 1945.

Saga of the Rhinos: A Brief History of the 748th Tank Battalion. 1945. Yeide, Harry. *Steel Victory: The Heroic Story of America's Independent Tank Battalions at War in Europe.* New York: Random House, 2003.

Partial Index

CPSIA information can be obtained at www.ICGtesting.com
Printed in the USA
BVOW08s2219200516

448949BV00001B/55/P